To Dwight,
with appre-
for all you
your Life — Leah
2003

I Am My Mother's Memory

I Am My Mother's Memory

Leah Pettepiece

Copyright © 2002 by Leah Pettepiece.

Library of Congress Number: 2002094869
ISBN :   Hardcover   1-4010-7700-5
              Softcover   1-4010-7699-8

All rights reserved. No part of this book may be reproduced or transmitted in any form or by any means, electronic or mechanical, including photocopying, recording, or by any information storage and retrieval system, without permission in writing from the copyright owner.

This book was printed in the United States of America.

To order additional copies of this book, contact:
Xlibris Corporation
1-888-795-4274
www.Xlibris.com
Orders@Xlibris.com
16321-PETT

⇝ Dedication

There are many stories in the world, for each persons life there is something worth the telling. I had never thought that I would write a book, never set out to be an author, until I married my husband Theo, who over the years of our marriage convinced me that the tales of my youth were worth the telling. So it is that I dedicate this book to him, with deep gratitude for his unswerving devotion, love and patience. There are many other people to whom I also owe a debt of thanks; to Brian Sketch who was my first editor and became not only a friend but a fellow searcher on the road to find the past; my step brother Tom who reminds me always of who I was; my dear friend Sadie Lynette without whose friendship and motherly support I might not have been able to persevere; to my daughter Mary who reminds me all the time that I am important because I carry the memories of our family; to my niece Chrissy who cheered me on and continues to be a support; to my son Devin and his wife Patti and to my grandson Tyler who I hope will someday understand the importance of each life.

I also want to thank the editors, Lovelia Laping and Stephen

Llevares and the staff at Xlibris who helped make my book a reality.

Last I dedicate this work to the many souls who have lost their lives to war, or hatred or prejudice, or acts of terrorism no matter what race, or creed, or nationality, and to those who survive them let me say this:

Remember, they are never lost to this earthly realm until the last person who remembers them is gone!

I Am My Mother's Memory

In Memory
Born September 16, 1896
Moscow, Russia
Died December 10, 1974
San Francisco, California

Chapter I

I Am My Mother's Memory

This is the story of a remarkable life, not the kind of soap opera stuff that you might find in the movies but a real down-to-earth one; this is how we lived its story. When I was a child growing up and someone, a teacher or the like, asked, "Where were you born, Elizabeth?" I would reply, "On a boat." The room would break out in laughter! You can imagine the scene, me trying to explain to someone who had never even been across the Brooklyn bridge and who had spent their whole lives right where they are now that I was born on a boat at sea in the middle of the Atlantic Ocean, coming from the nightmare that was the Second World War. Well . . . "You have to forgive them," my mother would say . . . "They don't have a very big view of life."

Well it's fifty-four years later and you know what? Mother was right. Not just then but even now, if someone asks and I answer . . . well, there is either total silence or a low, surly laugh! What? Was no one ever born on a boat? Well, at least now I'm old enough to not care, so that's how this story begins.

Like most people before the advent of artificial insemination and test tube babies, my life began without much pomp or circumstance. My mother and father lived in a small village in the part of the world then known as Slovakia. They had two boys and a baby girl. The war was on; the Nazi front moved closer daily; they struggled, according to my older brother, everyday, just to survive; but they found time to do what comes naturally and so I got on my way — a tiny little spirit flitting through space to occupy the embryo in my mother's womb.

From this point on the story loses its sense of humor, as things in that place and time were very difficult. My mother, who survived the awfulness of the Holocaust, never would talk to me about all that she went through so over the course of my lifetime I have had to piece together as best I could what happened. One day in the late fall of 1944 the Nazis came and took away all the men and young boys from the village and surrounding area; they were gathered up "like animals."

My older brother shared this with me years after Mother had died, when the information available enabled me to find him. The villagers were all Jewish and the surrounding area was filled with gypsies. Not wanting to bother with infants, the Nazis simply killed them on the spot, either by shooting them or by hanging them from the eaves of the barns. They literally slaughtered dozens of babies that afternoon, among them my sister and several cousins. My mother and her sister had walked to a nearby village to trade for food and came back to find that their village had been ravaged by a large group of Nazi soldiers as they pushed their way toward the Tatra Mountains in pursuit of the last remaining partisan units who had gone into hiding there. They found their little daughters among those in the barn, dead. Their sons and husbands had been loaded onto trucks and hauled away. A few of the Nazi soldiers had stayed behind and were beginning to round up the women. Just before sunset they and the rest of the women were loaded up and taken to a cattle station where they were held for several days before being loaded onto freight cars for the longest journey of their lives.

They never saw the men or the boys from the village again. At the end of their journey was Auschwitz; it was November 1, 1944. The shock of their internment was immense, at first it blocked out all feeling but grief; eventually it permeated their very souls just as the frost of the winter permeated the ground. Day in and day out, for most of that winter, the smell of burning flesh hung over the barracks. They were forced to work for the Nazis; tasks such as carrying those who had died during the night out to the trenches became commonplace. My aunt used to say that in the darkness of the night the low murmur of women's voices repeating the Kaddish over and over wore a groove into her mind. My mother was forced to work in the infirmary; there she witnessed unthinkable cruelties and often watched helplessly as prisoners begged for death to take them from the horror of it all. My aunt worked in the kitchen and sometimes stole potato skins or other items which had been disposed of by their captors, hiding whatever she dared in the folds of her undergarments, to take back to the barracks and share with the other women.

Somehow, miraculously both of them survived. When the end of the war came and the camps were liberated, my mother, who was pregnant, and my aunt were sent to a camp for displaced persons and then slotted quickly on to America.

This is where my real story begins. I was born on the ship deck of a Finnish ship, the *Helga*, one of many ships mobilized to bring survivors to the United States. Per the records of the ship's captain I weighed in on a fish scale at a mere five lbs. Being a good man and fearful for the life of his new little passenger, he moved my mother, myself and my aunt to his steward's room and put me in a drawer with "plentiful plaid wool shirts" to ensure that I would not freeze. In the ship's log I was not given a name, only "baby Jew girl" . . . and a note: "Mother refused to name the baby, stating that it was no use as the child would probably die." I wasn't given a name until we reached America.

When we arrived in Ellis Island there was much to do before we were given entrance to New York, and in the process of the health inspections my mother was found to have tuberculosis.

Because of this she was sent back on the same vessel. My aunt took responsibility for me and no one seemed to notice. So I came to be my aunt's child. When she registered me she named me Elzpeth, but the lady who was documenting my registration was of another nationality and so the name was spelled Elizabeth. We were assigned to a special section of the city when we finally went ashore and were given a small apartment paid for by the benevolence of some aristocratic New York Jews. All these years later, I still have memories of the building that was my first home. It towered into the gray sky and our front window looked down onto the street. There was a small grocer downstairs and a pickle lady next door.

The times that I remember were hard. There was never enough to eat and often, late at night, I would hear my mother crying and talking to herself in Yiddish. Often I would fall off to sleep with the sound of her desperate, anguished crying. At times I would get out of my bed and go to her but she always sent me away, whispering, "It's nothing, child, nothing. Only my memories."

We lived in the tenement district of the lower east side of New York, and to hear some of the stories that come from there you'd think it was all wonderful and romantic, but for me it was lonely and sad. I could never really tell why but there was this gnawing, empty hole inside of me that made me feel uncared for and unloved. We kept to ourselves except for the synagogue. It was a tiny storefront-type building. Inside, there were great wonders for a small girl. I loved to go there on Friday nights and felt as if it was the one place in all creation where I truly belonged. My fondest memory was of a neon star of David that hung from the ceiling across from the women's section upstairs. I loved to peer at it and wondered how it came to be there.

My mother, I am sure, tried to care for me the best that she could, but I don't have any memories of feeling loved. In fact the opposite is true. I have a recurring nightmare that has been with me all my life. It comes to haunt me when I am sad or ill. In the dream I am very small. I am tied in a high chair with a cloth around my waist so that I can't get away. The chair is facing a window with light streaming through, which slowly turns to darkness. There is a cup from which I drink all the milk. I get cold and frightened . . . I am wet . . . I cry but no one comes to rescue me . . . I am alone!

I remember that Mother would often not allow me close to her; she would shove me away or lock me in the tiny closet of the kitchen where, from the darkness, I would hear her crying and pounding her fists on the wall. As I grew older I learned to notice when she was having a bad day and to stay outside as much as I could. Sometimes I would go down to the pickle lady who was kind and very loving. She would take me inside and tell me stories; sometimes she would feed me sandwiches smothered in sweet butter made of liverwurst or cheese. Mrs. Morgenstern was a robust lady with the tinges of gray in her hair that come at the beginning of old age. She had big hands and an even bigger heart. She wore a wig and was always adjusting it. I used to wonder if she was bald underneath. She loved all the children in the neighborhood. She gushed over how thin I was and always insisted that I have a pickle. To this day, whenever I open a jar of Bubbies Kosher Dills, my heart warms and I remember. So I managed to be out of the way whenever Mother was upset, oftentimes by visiting in the pickle shop. I always felt afraid when she took to singing in Yiddish or mumbling to herself because I knew that what came next would be the endless tears and her anger.

My mother had met a young U.S. soldier at the relocation camps and when he arrived back home in the states he was billeted in New York. He found us through the logs on Ellis Island and whenever he could he would visit us, usually bringing me fruit and bringing food to Mother. Slowly, he courted her; he even tried to learn Yiddish. I remember laughing when he tried to say things to me, and he would smile and give me a hug and say, "When you learn English . . ." And I did begin to learn, quickly, because I thought that it was important. My mother said, "New country . . . New language . . . New life." It became a motto in our apartment. Life wasn't all bad, life was just hard. Even the community about us who were our own people looked at us strangely . . . except for . . . well, Mrs. Morgenstern, the pickle lady, who learned that I loved dill pickles like most kids love sweets. She would call to me, "Leah, little Kindalah . . . come and have a pickle." And she would let me choose from the great round glass jar. "Ahh," she'd gush and give me a little hug. I should be so lucky. And there was the Rabbi who came round to check on all of us who were "new" to America. He was the most wonderful, kind man. He would look at me so hard that I wanted to hide. He would talk in Yiddish with my mother and always in low, fast tones that I couldn't understand. Always before he left he would spend a few moments with me. He would pat my curls and smile. He gave me a dime each time he came. For a long time the dimes went into mother's purse but eventually they went into a little pouch he gave me made of red velvet. I saved them for many years. Whenever I took them out to look at them I could see the Rabbi's eyes smiling softly at me; it made me feel loved and cared for.

Then one spring day in the middle of my fourth year of life, the young man who had been courting my mother came to visit. He asked me if I thought I would like to have a father. Well . . . I never had one, so what was I to say? My mother smiled all over. When he had gone she explained that she was going to marry Mr. McRyan. "It will make a better life for us, and you will be protected." I wasn't sure just what she meant by that but I did know that I liked Mr. McRyan very much, not just for the presents he brought us but because he noticed things, like the time my shoes were too small. He took me on a walk down to the cobbler and bought me new ones without my asking!

One morning in early June, Mr. McRyan came for us. He wasn't wearing his uniform anymore and he was driving a shiny black car. All the neighborhood came out to see us off. The pickle lady cried. She hugged me tightly and whispered something in Yiddish that I didn't understand. I wondered what would become of us. I had never been farther out of our neighborhood than the Post Office on Broom St. I was excited but frightened. I got real sick to my stomach riding in the back seat of the car and started to cry. Mr. McRyan pulled right over and took me out to get some air. He explained that it was all right and not to be anxious, everything was going to be fine. I felt out of place and lost, all the words in the world weren't going to make me feel any better. Mother scolded me when we got back into the car, which made it even more frightening.

We traveled by car a long way into the night. I will never forget the ride for two very simple reasons: first, of course, because I got car-sick, but mostly because I was amazed that one could travel and come to a place where there were suddenly no big, tall buildings and instead there was sky as far as you could see and horses behind little fences like in the storybook at school. I'm sure that the trip took so long because every time I said, "Oie, look!" or "Look, *look!*" Mr. McRyan would pull off to the side of the road and we'd climb out and, as he put it, "Have a good look." I got very tired finally after it turned dark. When I woke we were at Mr. McRyan's brother Ed's house. There was so much to eat that I got sick all over again. Later my new aunt Bette fed me again. She said, "Now if you just take it slow, and only eat a bit, it'll be okay." Well I heeded her advice and fell right in love with fried chicken. It was my first experience with anything so grand. The little corn biscuits were like angel food to me. Next morning, when we were getting ready to leave, Aunt Bette gave me a little box with all sorts of goodies in it and most especially corn bread!

There was another whole day of travel and by now my mother looked a little scared herself. I noted that she was very quiet and so did Mr. McRyan, so the two of us tried to make up for it. We stopped and saw everything that day. I got to see my first cow face to face, we waded in a creek to cool our feet, and I gathered flowers from the edge of a meadow for my mother. I loved the countryside, I felt free and happy. Finally at late evening we arrived in Chicago. When we drove into the city I was a little worried because I was real fond of being able to see things. Mr. McRyan told me that I shouldn't fuss, that he didn't plan for us to live here nor in fact in any city. "No sir," he said matter-of-factly. "My little girl isn't going to do without fresh air."

We stayed several days in Chicago and I was often left with a nurse. That puzzled me because I'd never been left with anyone, but Mother said that this was how things were to be and that I would just have to get along. And get along I did; poor nurse, I had her running in circles. First to the fountain in the lobby then off to see the bears and dolls at the department store near the hotel, then round to the park at the center of the street! Finally our stay there ended and we were back on the road out in the country. I had already begun to formulate a strong desire to live "out in the country" from our travels so far. Little did I know that my soon-to-be father had a mother or that she lived in the country by a lake. There would be many apprehensive moments in my young life, times when I felt alone and forlorn. Sometimes I was incredibly happy for the life given to me by my stepfather and fate, but there also were times when I felt unloved and unwanted and believed that the world was a harsh, even cruel, place where everyone only loved you if you were perfect!

There was however in my life one steady immoveable force. Her name was Becka Arthur McRyan-Find a Doe. Can you imagine such a name? She was my Romanian-gypsy step—grandmother. A feast at once for the eyes and the soul of a child like myself, she stood about five-foot-four and had eyes of ebony and thick, dark mahogany brown hair. When she smiled it was as if her whole face became animated. Her skin was soft and smooth, the color of tanned leather.

She had traveled to the United States on a Conestoga wagon with her seventeen-year-old sister when their parents and her sister's husband died in a flu epidemic in Canada. She was only fifteen at the time. To me she was remarkable! Strong of body, strong of opinion, strong of almost anything you can imagine! Had it not been for her, my life, I am convinced, would have been *hell*!

The first time that I laid eyes on her was at the wedding of my mother to my stepfather. My mother and I had lived in a hotel in the dells in Wisconsin for the two weeks prior to the wedding and though many of my soon-to-be aunts came to visit and to help with the preparations, she did not!

My mother said in private that it was because we were Jews and she was a Roman catholic, whatever that meant. In public, when she was mentioned by my stepfather's sisters, she was portrayed as busy with all the cooking needed for the huge reception that would follow the wedding. With such little information, was it any wonder that a five-year-old was terrified when on the night before the wedding, as Mother tucked me into bed, she told me that I would be spending the next four weeks with this new grandmother whom I had not even seen and who I imagined to be someone like the witch in the Hansel and Gretel book my stepfather loved to read to me! I didn't sleep all night. I cried and worried, until morning light came through the blinds in the windows.

When at last we were all dressed for the wedding I felt exhausted and scared, not to mention nearly ready to run away! My new aunties had bought me a beautiful yellow-and-white dress that made a soft tinkling noise when I walked and little patent leather shoes, but I didn't feel cute or pretty as my stepfather said. I felt all out of place; I had never been so dressed up. The shoes were hard and clicked along when I stepped, and oh, it was difficult to go down the stairs with my new stepdad. His sister Maude was my mother's bridesmaid and I was her flower girl. We had practiced in the great hall of the hotel many times what to do, but when we got inside the door and I saw everything so splendid, I didn't remember a thing and Aunt Maude had to whisper to me. Soon I had made my way to the front, strewing the rose petals in my basket, but not quite all of them. Secretly I wanted to keep a few; I had seen flowers in the streets of New York in the stalls run by girls in pinafores but never ever had I had any of my own. I don't recall how the service got on but suddenly the Rabbi was calling to me to come to my new father and then I remember exactly that he promised that nothing would befall me that he could stop and as long as he lived he would protect me and care for me as his own child. Well suddenly I felt like the world just opened up and swallowed me whole. What did it all mean?

Later, as we finished eating, a real gypsy band came around to our table where I sat between my mother and new father. As they began to play, my father took my mother to the dance floor and suddenly I was alone . . . but not for long. From a table off to our left came a tall, beautiful woman dressed in a silk blouse with a million ruffles and a skirt made of quiltwork in gay colors. She had a braid as big around as my arm and it hung down her shoulder over her bosom to below her waist. It had bright-colored ribbons in it. When she got right up to me she swept me up in her strong brown arms and hugged me so close that I thought I would faint. She smelled like the forest: pine and evergreen, moss and peat, damp and cool.

"You are mine now," she whispered, "and I shall never let you go!" Then she whirled us both out on to the dance floor and I realized that she had bells on her skirt that tinkled like fairy bells when she moved. Her grip loosened and she looked at me hard as we twirled round and round. "Don't be afraid," she whispered, "I am your grandmamma now, and you . . . why, you are my only granddaughter." I was at once at ease and convinced beyond the shadow of a doubt that my mother was wrong! How could someone who looked like one of the fairies in my story book be right here, holding me in her arms and dancing across the floor to the beat of the gypsy band as if she had known me forever? Well certainly she was not to be feared and for the first time that I can remember I actually knew I was loved beyond a doubt and that this person into whose control I had fallen would never hurt me or let anyone else. From that moment on she cherished and protected me. Much later in my life, when I caused my stepfather to become angry with me, she became the one person I could depend on to take up my cause. She was always there for me.

⇝ Chapter II

Life for me from this point on would never quite be the same simple affair that it was in the confines of New York. I found myself utterly taken with my new grandmother and felt not the least afraid, in fact life with her was an adventure in itself. The morning after the wedding my mother and new father set out on a trip, and I boarded the train to travel with my grandmother to Mason Lake, Wisconsin, to a farm in the beautiful woods near the dells. It was wonderful; we traveled by train for a while and then by car from the station in the country out to "the Lake" as my grandmother called it.

When we turned off the paved road onto a narrow gravel road, I could not imagine what lay ahead. This was really out in the country, and I stood up on the back seat to see everything. The road turned again and again. On all sides there were beautiful trees and I recognized the smell of my new grand mother in the air.

At last the road made a long gradual turn and there ahead of us was a grand two-story house, white with bright blue-green trim. Lace curtains peeked out from the windows and the door was lit with a bright piece of stained glass: it looked like I was peering through a kaleidoscope!

When the car stopped, I jumped out and ran toward the house. I was so excited; I had never lived in a house.

My trip to the front door was quickly interrupted by a large black dog. He ran toward me as if he would eat me right there. I turned and ran back toward the car; too late, he knocked me to the ground and started to lick my face while my uncle Fred and Grandmother roared with laughter.

I was too scared to realize that he was just being friendly until my Uncle Fred regained his composure and hauled the dog off me. I began to cry. "It's all right," Grandma and Uncle Fred said. "Don't cry, Blackie loves children."

When finally I returned to my senses, the house beckoned and I headed more slowly in the direction of the door. Blackie came around again and, as calmly as calm could be, walked beside me, wagging his tail.

The house at the lake has lived forever etched in my memory as I saw it that first day — magical, beyond my imagining. This must have been one of those indelible moments for my brain because as I write this I can still see each little detail: the staircase inside, which wound its way up to the second floor; the beautiful woven rugs of all colors; the windows with their bright panels and starched lace curtains; most of all, the stained-glass window in the entry door.

Grandmother led me upstairs, careful to point out that her room was right next to mine. My room was perfect for a little girl. The bed had a bright gingham, pink lace and ribbon canopy; the bed itself was covered by a patchwork quilt that had more colors of pink in it than I knew existed. Grandmother explained that this used to be the room where the baby of the family slept, and now it would be mine. The dresser held a pitcher in a basin on a marble top and the mirror stood on the floor. There was a beautiful doll on the bed with a note in her pocket. Grandmother read me the note: "To my new granddaughter, this is for all the Christmastimes that you never had a toy." I kept the note for years. At the time I didn't know what Christmas was all about —

Mother and I were Jews and this was new to me — but I loved that doll.

I was so excited that I couldn't keep still. I kept asking questions about everything. Why, if there was running water at the kitchen sink, did we have to go outside to an "outhouse?" How did one take a bath if there was no bathroom? Why did grandmother have an icebox in the house but when dinner time came she had to go to the "root cellar" to get potatoes and carrots?"

Grandmother was very patient with me. "You'll come to understand it all," she'd tell me. "Take your time to learn everything, we have a whole month." I had thought that the food we ate at the reception was wonderful, but dinner my first night alone with Grandmother was much better. She fixed roast venison; as I was unacquainted with deer meat, you can imagine all the questions I had about that. Alongside the meat were mashed potatoes and thick brown gravy, homemade biscuits and steamed carrots.

Later, after we did the dishes, Grandmother took me for a little adventure down to the edge of the lake to an old mill. "Look down in the little pool at the end of the mill," she whispered. What I saw took my breath away: There was the big full moon, reflected just like a picture. I would often come here on my own in future years and try to scoop up the water in my hands so that I could catch the moon.

When bedtime came, Grandmother gave me a glass of warm milk and some apple cookies, then she tucked me into the big bed and invited me to say my prayers. "But, Grandmother, I don't know any," I whispered. She knelt then by my bed, put her wonderful big hands over mine and began to sing. When she finished, the room felt so quiet. "What did the words mean?" I begged. She told me that it was an Indian prayer for the safekeeping of a child. "I didn't think it would be right to say a Christian prayer," was all she said, giving me a kiss goodnight.

Every day at the lake was an adventure. Grandmother took me to the reservation nearby when she went to tend a sick old lady, and she taught me to speak in their language to say hello and goodbye. The Indians loved her and as a consequence they loved me too. The old lady that Grandmother treated on our first visit to the reservation was Ella White-cloud. "How did you get your name?" I asked her. "It was the first thing my mother saw after giving birth to me" was her reply.

I asked Ella if I could have an Indian name. "One day I will whisper in the wind a name for you," she told me. The chief of the tribe wanted to meet me, so when we left Ella we went up a little hill to a tiny little cabin. There were puppies in the yard, all spotted and cute. Grandmother introduced me to Chief Red Cloud and I said, "I know, you got your name from a cloud your mother saw." He laughed at me and sent me to play with his grandson Charlie and the puppies.

First thing I wanted to know was how come Charlie didn't have a special name. He frowned, "I'm only a half-breed." "What's that?" I asked as politely as I could. "I ain't got no father who's Indian," he stated simply.

I told him I was sorry. "It's alright, let's play with the pups," he said. He asked where I got my name and I told him it was a Hebrew name. When he asked where I was born and I told him on a boat, he didn't laugh, instead he looked off toward the lake and said, "If I had been born on the lake I would have gotten a water name." At once we were friends; we had great fun with the pups and we tumbled about in the sweet-smelling grass together.

I had never seen puppies before except in a picture book, so this to me was great fun! When grandmother was ready to leave, the Chief came out where we were playing. "Would you like a pup?" he asked. "Would I?" "Grandmother, could I?" "I told the chief it was all right if you took one, but you know it will have to live here with me when you go, but it will still always be your pup." I thought that was a grand idea. Charlie helped me pick: a little girl-pup who was smaller than the others. "She'll be a real nice friend for you," he said. So I carried home my first present from the reservation, a brown-and-black-spotted pup, half coyote and half spaniel.

Grandmother insisted that I pick a name for the pup right

away. I wasn't too familiar with names for dogs so she gave me endless suggestions until I decided that I would call her Spot!

During that month I would learn so much: how to find the right herbs for the stew Grandmother would make, how to tell if a berry was ripe before I plucked it from the bush; how big a sunfish has to be before it's big enough to eat; how to fish; how to swim with no clothes on in the lake under the moonlight.

I ate and played and grew to love this place called "Grandmother's" and I grew to love her too. Never during that month was I homesick. Everyone had talked about how I would "probably be homesick"; well, whatever it was, I wasn't. I didn't miss my mom or even think about the time. When at last the month was at an end, and grandmother told me that my mom and dad would be there tomorrow, I was sad.

The morning that my mom and dad were to arrive was very busy. Grandmother had cleaned house the whole day before and done laundry and made a wonderful bunch of "goodies." She gave me a bath in the big galvanized tub that I had come to love. She parted my hair in the middle and braided it full of beads the way she wore hers, and then she gave me a big surprise: a pair of hand-beaded moccasins from Charlie's mom and a dress made out of hide, stained white with wonderful beads and bells on it. When I looked in the mirror, I squealed with delight. "Mother won't know me, she'll think I'm a little Indian girl!"

Grandmother laughed and her laughter filled my soul with mirth. She was so much a part of me now; I even knew the Indian prayer for sleeping! I was so sorry that my time at the lake was going to end . . . "Little one, you fret too much," she gently scolded me. "You'll be here every summer, just you wait, and other times too you'll come here."

I wasn't sure that my mother would let me but I believed in my Grandmother and if she promised I knew it was "written in stone," an Indian phrase I had picked up. I was glad to see my mother and my stepfather.

We stayed on at the lake for another week. My mother liked Grandma, I could tell. They spent a lot of time together in the kitchen, cooking, sharing recipes, and talking. On our last night there, Mother made chicken dinner. It was really wonderful; I didn't know that she could cook so well. I suppose that she didn't have the money or the food to make such a nice meal back in New York.

My stepfather had arranged for us to have a house in the outskirts of Washington, D.C. He had decided that it would be best because the schools there were better and it was not as rushed and crowded as the city. I wanted very much to take Spot but my mother didn't want me to, so Grandmother said that she would keep her for me until I came again in the summer.

To my surprise Mother thought that it would be a good idea for me to visit as often as time allowed. Grandmamma looked sad the morning that we packed up to go to our new home. I felt strange inside, not that I didn't want to be with my mother and stepfather, just that here in this place I felt a security and love that I had never had before. I cried when we were saying goodbye, it was the first time in my young life that I had become attached, bonded to someone else. Grandmamma held me tight and whispered, "You'll be back often, little one. You mustn't make your mother feel bad." I dried my tears and tried to be brave but I really wanted just to stay there forever in the magical confines of the great old farm house with the dogs, the lake and the gentle sighing of the pines as the wind passed through.

I stared out the back window of the car as we drove off until I couldn't see the house anymore. Grandmamma stood on the front porch peering after us, waving.

Chapter III

Looking back, one always sees things more clearly than when we pass through them the first time. We left the lake and I had my new father's promise that I would be back there when the summer came. Father had bought us a home in the outskirts of Washington, D.C. It was a rather plain house from the exterior but it was a wonderful warm house on the inside. There was a stairway that went up, both from the kitchen and from the entryway. The whole second floor of the house was wrapped around by a balcony with a banister of twisted dark mahogany wood; it formed a great high ceiling for the living room and dining room. My room was bright and flowery, there was wood up halfway on the wall and wallpaper with roses in shades of yellow up to the ceiling. There were two great dormer type windows with seats in them, which also served as chests to store things in. I had a canopy bed much like the bed at Grandmother's but of a dark tone with great knobs on the top of all four corners. My room opened into another room which Father called "the playroom" and beyond that there was yet another room where my nurse slept.

At first when my father said I was to have a nurse I protested,

"I'm not sick!" He laughed and I heard the remnants of my grandmother's laugh in his. "She will help to care for you until you are a bit older," came his easy explanation. The first nurse I remember was an English woman who insisted that I speak appropriately at all times. She worked hard to break the heavy accent I carried from the mix of languages in my early years

My days were very busy while we lived in the house on Lincoln Lane. I had cousins close by who weren't too sure about their new little relative but they were very nice to me because they said Grandmother would have a fit if they weren't. Well, it was difficult to adjust to the new surroundings and even more difficult to get used to the three cousins who came everyday to see me. The problem was that they were all older by at least eleven years and they were *boys*!

Whenever they thought up a new game I became the mom, or the Indian maiden or the shop lady or some other feminine role, but I wanted to be a cowboy or an Indian and join in the great romps through the yards or slide down the banister on the stairs like they did. Secretly I loved having them come . . . oh how quickly I learned things that helped me to get on with other kids in the neighborhood. Often while we lived there I would find my mother crying in her room or staring speechless out the windows . . . I would ask if she was all right and usually she would answer in Yiddish, "No, but it doesn't matter."

I started school the next year. I remember how proud I was when my father walked me to my classroom. My grandmother had sent me a dress she made just for the occasion. It was red plaid and had tiny little lace cuffs and a collar that was bright white; I felt pretty! I learned my first hard lesson that day: People don't believe things that they have no experience about. The teacher was a nice older lady with pretty blond hair and she talked to each of us alone then introduced us to the class. When she told the class that I had been born on a boat and was a refugee, everyone wanted to know what it was. She explained and then the rest of the kids acted standoffish; it hurt my feelings but I didn't say anything.

One other girl was a refugee, too. She was from Puerto Rico and now lived with her grandma because her mother had died. She and I had lots of things in common. We had trouble with our English, had deep accents and sometimes weren't understood. We also both had dark, thick curls and were smaller than our classmates. Soriata and I became friends. We played together in the playground; at times we laughed when we couldn't understand each other, and together we managed to not let the other kids' attitudes bother us.

Life settled into a routine by the end of the second year. I made friends and learned to do what all kids do in school: Survive no matter what! Just about this time my father's first wife, whom he had divorced, died and my two stepbrothers came into my life.

Chuck was great! He loved me right off, he would play with me, read to me and even help me with my homework. He was a kind, soft-spoken teenager. Edward at first didn't seem to care at all for me but I noticed that whenever I got into a problem with Mom, which seemed to be often, he always came to defend me, as if he thought she would hurt me. He would stand by and not say anything unless she said she was going to spank me and then he would fly into action taking the full blame for whatever infraction of the rules I had made. Mother never spanked him; she would get flustered by his antics and walk off, talking to herself in Yiddish.

Usually Edward disappeared too and I would have to find him to say thank you! My stepbrothers went to a private military school and when they were gone during the week the house seemed cold — you know the kind of lonely cold that seeps in when someone you love is away. I noticed that it happened too when Father was away at his work for the government.

Mother never talked to me when I was small except to tell me to eat or dress or not do something that she caught me at, like trying to climb upon a chair and get onto the banister to slide down, or eating in my room. My nurse whose name I have forgotten took care of me all the time. She helped me dress and bathe and would spend hours trying to work out my hair which was full of "rats" due to its being so curly. She stayed with us until I was seven. When it came time for her to leave, I felt the same coldness in the house.

Now I was alone with my mother while my brothers were in school and my father was away. The maid and the cook didn't live with us and nighttimes were something that I learned to fear. My mother often sang to herself in Russian or Yiddish and hardly ever spoke to me. She wouldn't read to me or help me bathe and one night when father came home late he found me in bed with my clothes still on. He helped me bathe, gave me hot chocolate, and put me in bed. And then I heard him talking to my mother in harsh tones and understood what she said to him in strident Yiddish: "She is *not* my child!" My heart felt like a stone, what did she mean, was she angry with me, did I do something to make her say that? All night I lay awake, trying to piece together why she might have said that.

When morning finally came my father appeared at breakfast to tell me that my mother was "ill" and would be going to a "hospital" later that day. He explained to me that I would have a nurse again soon and until then our cook had agreed to stay at night and help me with homework and get me ready for bed. He asked me if I knew what my mother said to him the night before and if I could tell him in English because she had refused to speak in English anymore. I didn't want to tell him; he said he understood if it was something that I didn't want to say, but that she had kept repeating it over and over and he just wondered what it was.

It would be years before I would tell him that she had said, "She is not my child." I, however, stopped wondering why she didn't like me, and oddly enough I stopped trying to please her, I decided that my father was going to take care of me as he had promised and that whatever kept her from caring wasn't going to make a difference to me.

Mother went to the hospital and there she stayed, for what seemed like a long time, but in reality only a couple of months.

When she returned home she seemed glad to be there, she made a fuss over me, and for a while she even acted like I was important . . . Until, one day, when we had been sitting in the garden and I had read to her from my school book and I felt safe and close, I decided to ask her why she had said I wasn't her child. I watched her face change color, going slowly white. She looked at me in a mix of what seemed to be sadness and anger.

"I never said that!" she said emphatically, then she rose from the bench, went into the house and started humming to herself in Yiddish. We never read another book together.

I learned the pain of a lie that day, the lesson has served me well through life. Others may lie to us, about us, and even attempt to make us lie . . . but the truth is a stronger force and eventually will win out. We are after all sentient beings, the lessons life gives us make us responsible for our actions and our words.

Summer came and with it came the welcome time with my grandmother and other cousins at the lake. My father began a ritual the first summer of my life with him that would continue through my lifetime, all the way to the eighth year of my daughter's life.

Summer meant many things, but most of all it meant magical moments spent in the company of Grandmother, who neither cared for shoes, nor yelled if you got dirty . . . who would in fact get dirty with you! I loved it. Freedom to be a child of the earth in the truest sense of the word. When I arrived at the lake, the first thing Grandmother always did was to take me to the back porch and let me pore through three big steamer trunks of clothing to find things that fit, then she would take me upstairs to my room and we would take my suitcase and put it up on the high shelf in the closet! "There," she would say when the deed was done, "now let's see if there is a real girl inside those city clothes." And off would come the tidy dress mother had sent me in, on would go the blue jeans, plaid shirt and sandals. "Ha, there you are!" she'd laugh, and summer would begin.

The woods around the house were magical. I loved to go pick

flowers or search for herbs and mushrooms with my grandmother. I loved the smell of the pine trees and the feel of the cool, damp earth under my feet. I climbed rocks, swam naked, fished for bluegill till dark ... and ate and grew in ways that one can't measure with a yardstick on the wall.

Together at the lake in the summer usually were the youngest of my still all-male horde of cousins. One day my grandma had to go into Madison for some things and she asked my cousin Warren to take me fishing with him. He had other ideas. He chased me until I went up on the roof of the coal shed and then he took the ladder down. He simply didn't want to take me along; he was meeting his friend Jay. Well, fortunately I knew not to try to jump off a six-foot-high roof. But, not to be undone, I spent the afternoon gathering up pieces of coal, and when I saw them walking back up the hill I threw such a barrage of stones that it cost Warren six stitches! Grandmother never said a word to me until the doctor left, then she made me apologize to Warren; afterwards she took him out on the back porch and paddled him for leaving me up there. Next morning, Warren took me fishing; he never told me she made him but I knew. Funny though; ever after that we were good friends — when his plane was shot down in Korea I cried for hours. Life has its way with us, we learn and stumble and get up and go on. We grow and stretch and move forward, propelled by an unseen force within us and the love of those around us. We survive, against all odds ... or maybe sometimes because of them.

I Am My Mother's Memory 33

Chapter IV

We lived on in the house on Lincoln Lane for three more years after Mother first went to the hospital. She continued to have times when she sang to herself in Yiddish or Russian, or sat and stared out the window, unspeaking. She also basically continued to ignore me, until one day in the spring of the year when I was in fourth grade. We were studying social history in school and had begun the stories of the Second World War. By now I knew some of the things that had happened because my stepfather often talked to me about the war, how he first met my mother and how we came to America. I recall that my teacher had asked me to ask my mother if she would come to our class to talk about what she had gone through. I of course was full of pride that the teacher would ask me to do this. My mother was sitting by the window, reading, when I got home. I quickly changed my clothes and then went quietly in to ask her. I was terrified of the question and it took me a while to get up the courage to speak. I just sat there until finally she looked over the top of her book and said simply, "Yes, what do you want?" I blurted out that my teacher wanted to know if she would come and talk to my class about the war and what happened to her.

Her eyes froze; they pierced right through me and for the first time in my life she struck out at me. The slap across my face was so quick that I felt as if I had been struck by lightning! I fell off the chair and before I could get up she was bending over me, screaming in Yiddish. So sharp were her words that I couldn't think fast enough to translate any of them except the last sentence: "First the Nazis take my life and now you want to put me on display!"

She left me there on the floor sobbing. she stepped right over me without even looking back. When my father got home I was still sitting in the living room on the wing chair, crying. After he heard my story he gathered me up in his arms and tried to help me understand that her anger wasn't at me, it was at the horrible things that had happened to her. He took me to the bathroom and washed my face with his big, gentle hands, combed my hair and straightened my barrettes. He took me to the kitchen and told Mrs. Brand to give me something to drink. He went up the back stairs and I heard him carefully close the door at the top.

Next morning my mother sat at the breakfast table with us but she neither spoke nor ate. She stared off as though she wasn't there at all. Father said that he would take me to school because he wanted to speak with my teacher.

In the afternoon when I came home I noticed that my mother was back in her chair by the living room window, reading again. I didn't go in but went quietly to my room and stayed there until I heard my father's cheery voice. "Hello, house, I'm home," he called out from the entryway. I flew down the stairs and he hugged me tight then held me out from him and asked in a hushed tone. "Are you all right?" I assured him that I was and that I certainly was glad he was home early. During dinner that night Father announced that he had a surprise for us: We would be leaving Washington because he had received and appointment as an Adjutant to the Ambassador to France. Mother never said a word; she rose from her place at the table and left us sitting there. I, on the other hand, made up for her silence; I asked a million questions but the most important of all was where would we live.

My father told me that he would have a leave of forty days before he had to go to France and that he had decided to move us out in the country near to his sister Hyacinth and her husband so that I would be near to family in case I should be lonely. I was . . . terrified! I didn't know how to tell him that I was afraid to be alone with my mother. Before I formulated the question he answered it. There would be a live-in cook and a maid who stayed at least during the week days. "You won't be alone, I promise," he told me, patting my hand.

The next two weeks were a blur of activity. We drove to Elgin, Wisconsin and quickly found a house. I liked it right away because it was white clapboard like Grandmother's and had beautiful yards surrounding it, with a pond in the back and several large oak trees right near the house. Mother said little but did seem to be in a better mode when she saw how lovely the new house was. There were great windows that looked out from every room and although the living room was not as grand as the one on Lincoln Lane it had a plus: There was a way to open the sliding wall between the sitting area and the living room to make it almost twice as big, and there were two beautiful crystal chandeliers that matched one in each room. The floors were hard wood and Mother loved them. She immediately asked if we could get a matched pair of Persian carpets for this area and of course my father said we would.

The furniture arrived from Lincoln Lane at the end of the third week and we were in by the Wednesday before my mother's birthday. Father invited all his relatives to come for dinner and it was grand. For the first time I realized that my mother was actually quite beautiful. When she came down the winding stairway to greet the guests there was an audible hush in the room; she looked like a princess. She wore a teal-colored gown that accented her tiny waist, and her hair was held up all around with a tiny set of combs with pearls on them.

I also realized that night that I loved her and that she never let me tell her that. It was the first time that I realized how much I needed her to approve of me, to care about me, to love me.

Soon it was time for my father to leave. I couldn't sleep the night before, and I cried and felt as if I wouldn't be able to stand it. I'm sure he knew, but he didn't say anything when at breakfast I couldn't eat and had to use my napkin to dab at my eyes. We went out to the train station in my Uncle Lloyd's car. My father hugged me tight and told me to be good and take care of my mother. I noticed that when he told my mother good-bye she only shrugged and said nothing. On the drive back to the house I heard her softly humming one of her Yiddish tunes to herself. It was nice to be where I could walk out of my backyard and be in the woods, able to escape the trapped feeling that descended.

It was also nice to be close by my Aunt Hyacinth. She was Grandmother's oldest daughter and her boys were all away at college, so I had her to myself when I went to visit. She was a wonderful lady who made the best cookies, pies and cakes in the world. During the next six months I would learn to bake from her and would learn how to write poetry.

Mother and I lived quietly there during the first absence of Father, and it would be nice if I could say that we learned to communicate but we didn't. In fact there were times in that house when we didn't even speak to each other for over a week. I don't know what I would have done if Cook hadn't been there or I hadn't been able to go to my aunt's home.

We always had a lot of books in our home and Father subscribed to several good magazines. One afternoon I came in to find my mother sitting on the floor amid a pile of torn magazine pages. "What's wrong?" I asked futilely, but she never responded. Cook said she had gotten the mail and given it to Mother and later she heard her crying and speaking in a strange language. When she went into the living room mother was tearing up the magazine. Days later I would make the discovery that the magazine had published pictures of the actual camp where my mother and her sister had been. Mother was ill in bed for over a week; she wouldn't eat, she wouldn't talk, and, when I would slip in to see her, she would tell me in Yiddish "Go away, I do not want to see your face!"

My aunt telegraphed my father and he arrived home in the middle of the second week. Mother went to the hospital and Father took a leave to be there with me. This time I was older; I asked lots of questions and my father and Dr. Ambrose tried to answer them for me. Father bought me things to read about how the war had affected people in Europe, and for the first time I realized that Mother couldn't love me. In fact I wondered if she loved Father.

When Mother was able she came home and Father went back to France. I knew that summer was coming and I would go up to the lake by train to be with my grandmother. So I began a diary —, not the sort of diary you'd expect from a girl my age but one full of the questions that I couldn't ask my mother. I knew that if my grandmother could she would answer them for me.

Mother was frail; she was white as a ghost and thin as a rail. She paced and talked almost not at all. She spoke to me at meals and at bedtime but she never engaged in real conversation, at least not with me. Father had found a German Jewish lady who spoke Yiddish to come in twice a week and visit with my Mother. At these times she would be animated and engaging. Often the lady would spend hours with her, sometimes staying for dinner. I liked Mrs. Stein too, she always took time to talk to me for a while and one day she asked if I would like to go to synagogue with her. I hadn't been to one since we left New York and I was curious, so I went.

I was enthralled; the sanctuary itself was beautiful and, unlike in the synagogue of my early childhood, the women sat in the main part of the building with the men. The Rabbi was a nice, jolly fellow with a gray beard, and he quickly invited me to attend Hebrew School on Saturdays. Next morning bright and early I was up and dressed as if for school. Mother asked if I forgot it was Saturday and when I told her that I intended to walk to Sabbath School, she actually smiled. "I'll ask Cook to drive you," she told me. So it was that my formal training in my Judaic beliefs began, and I learned a new lesson from life: There is a thread that runs through all of us that makes us yearn for a greater self, some mystical tie that binds us to a Creator, whatever we might envision that to be, and once we begin to seek Him, great things open to us! I loved regular school and soon enough I loved Hebrew School as well. Not only would I be able to ask about my heritage but also I would finally begin to get answers that no one had given me before.

Hebrew School was the first place that I felt totally accepted by my peers. When I told them I was born on a boat coming to the U.S. after my mother and her sister had lived through the camps, no one laughed, the teacher squeezed me tight, and all my classmates were instantly my friends! It was balm to my aching spirit and a blessing to my little soul.

I convinced my mother that she would love the little synagogue and so it was that on the next Friday evening when I went down to eat, the table was set differently; there were candles glowing brightly. I heard Mrs. Stein's voice in the kitchen, and when the door swung opened there was my mother. She was in a black silk dress with a tiny little lace collar and had a lace shawl over her shoulders. Her hair was pinned up with her pearl combs and she was actually smiling.

"Good Shabbat, Lepchen," she said as she passed me with the bread tray under a beautiful, dark blue cloth. "Come eat and then we'll go to Shul," said Mrs.Stein. And so it was that another great door opened in my life — I learned about Shabbat!

I was so proud that evening walking in to the temple; everyone wanted to meet my mother. My teacher, the Rabbi, and Mrs. Leiberman who taught Hebrew were all speaking to my mother in Yiddish. Later Mrs. Stein would tell me that she had asked my mother to go before but it wasn't until I asked that she said yes. My heart was bursting with pride!

So we passed the rest of the time until summer came. My mother still didn't speak to me but at least on Fridays and Saturdays she smiled at me and gave me a little hug when I went off to Shul for my studies. It seemed that we had at last found a commonality that if nothing else gave us time together that was pleasant and good.

≽ Chapter V

As soon as I got off the train in Madison, my Grandmother knew there was something up. I clutched my diary under my arm, and when she asked if she could carry it I said "no." She smiled in the way she did when she thought one of us cousins were up to something.

After the usual exchange of clothing on the back steps and my own rush inside to change into what I now referred to as my country clothes, I grabbed up the diary and ran down the back stairs to find her. She was sitting on an oak log in the backyard, feeding her newest pet, a raccoon, while Blackie and Spot lay off to the side, watching with rather disgruntled looks on their faces.

She looked up when I came out the back screen door. "Come here, meet Moses," she beckoned. Going to her, I noticed that she seemed just the same; it seemed somehow that age didn't change her. Magic! I thought to myself and made a mental note to ask her how to stay always young of face.

I sat down beside her and she offered the little raccoon to me. "I found him in the outhouse the other morning. He looked scrawny and I figured he'd got lost from his mom so we'd better help out." She was like that; there must have been thirty different animals there during my lifetime that grew into adulthood only because of her. Some, like the three deer, still came to be fed time and again.

"Grandmother," I began, "I was wondering, what do you know about the War, the Second World War?" She eyed me up and down with her deep experienced look. "What troubles you?" she asked. I silently laid my diary on her lap. She picked it up, looked at the first few pages, and stood up. "I know that it was horrid, beyond that it was evil, the things it did to people . . . but I know too that it was wonderful. Look in the mirror at yourself, you are so unique and special . . . you are born up out of the ashes of your people, like a phoenix bird! Will you let me read this through and through, then I'll begin to help you sort out the parts that are important to know."

I agreed and so began a long, deep summer at the lake, a time when I would learn the ways of God according to my grandmother and the horrors that man can force upon other men for no other reason than the fact we look different.

In all my young life there had been no tragedy that directly affected me, but the second morning I was there I could hear a great commotion down toward the old mill. By the time I ran to see what was wrong, it was too late! One of the neighbor's boys and his brother had been fooling around at the far end of the old mill and the younger one had slipped on the rocks, falling into what had once been the storage tank. He died there, right before our eyes, with my grandmother trying to hold together the back of his skull. I was too shocked to cry! I stood there frozen, looking at death! The boys' mother and my grandmother had tried to stem the flow of blood but the gash was so deep that there was nothing they could do.

A pall hung over the rest of us youngsters for days afterward. Grandmother took us into the dells to the funeral. She said it would help if we said good-bye. I recall that I couldn't stand the smell — there were so many flowers in the church — and that I felt sick the whole time. When it was over I felt relieved. We got back to the house and I changed clothes and took a walk all the way to Stand Rock. I climbed up the back of the tall, damp stones and sat up there for a long while, looking out across the river and the lake. We never stopped talking about that accident. The men who lived around the lake got together and built a high fence around the storage bin so that nothing could ever happen there again.

My grandmother began to answer my questions. Slowly she shared all that she knew about the Nazis and their killing of so many. She found a lady in the dells who knew firsthand what it was like — she was a refugee survivor of Buchenwald and her name was Sadie Katz. Grandmother took me to visit her. She was lovely, a little older than my mother. She had dark, curly hair like mine and fine snappy black eyes. She dressed in black. She wasn't sure that she was doing the right thing talking with me and often would say, "I wish your mother would tell you these things!"

I spent many afternoons with Sadie during that summer. She told me about the way they were hauled off from their home, how she lost her whole family — three children and her husband, her sister, sister-in-law and niece, how she thought that death would be easier than staying alive but that she said G-d sent her a dream and commanded her to live to tell what she had gone through. Sadie went all over speaking to schools, community groups, and to those in Christian groups who wanted to know. After I had been meeting with her for a while she showed me her arm where the Nazis had tattooed her and let me look through a box she had with her papers and the old stained yellow star with which she had been first marked while still living in the ghetto before the camp.

I received more education from Sadie and my grandmother that summer than I could have gotten in a lifetime of reading books about the subject. Most of my questions found their own answers before I even asked them and I gained a new view of my mother. I now felt something I was not acquainted with before: pity.

More changes came to my life that summer. I grew two inches, and my feet grew too. Up until now I had always been small for my age. Sadie said that I was growing because of the things I was learning and Grandmother said that Mother Nature just decided to give me a spurt!

Most of my cousins by this time had outgrown the lake, having become teenagers, so there were only three of us there that year. Everett, Jean, Aunt Lillian's twins, and myself. They were nice and not at all rowdy. It was different to be there with so few kids, and my inner self was growing too so that I wanted time to think and be alone and read and watch life.

Often after I had been to visit Sadie I would go out to Stand Rock. One afternoon I was sitting up there all alone, wondering what made some people able to bear the tragedies of life while others folded under the weight of them, when suddenly from nowhere came an eagle. His wings spread out near as long as I could reach with my arms outstretched. I had heard stories of how the eagles could carry off a small child but I knew that I was in no danger. At first he circled out over the lake and back toward me, as if trying to get a good look at whatever this was sitting on the top the rocks. Then he swooped right down toward me, coming within reach. I caught my breath He was beautiful, with gold eyes and brown and white feathers. I could hear the swish his wings made; he was that close to me. What strength, I thought, what elegance, what courage, to be able to lift your whole self above the ground and fly. One day, I promised myself, one day I'll learn to fly. I watched him and he watched me for a long while. I got a better understanding of what it is that makes one a survivor from that eagle: A survivor must have strength and courage like an eagle to be able to rise above whatever comes in life and go on in elegance.

My grandmother and I always made lots of trips up to the reservation while I was there. She would go to take eggs to the chief or to tend someone's injury or illness. The day after I saw the eagle we went to visit Ella, and as soon as she saw me she whispered, "Eagle Spirit." At first I thought I was imagining what she said but then she put one hand on each of my shoulders and looked me straight in the eye.,"Eagle Spirit," she said again! An Indian name, but how could she possibly know . . . "You sat with the Eagle, it shows in your eyes," she told me. "I did,yesterday . . . out at Stand Rock," I replied. " I know," was her only reply.

Once again life surprised me with its way of wrapping around; why, I wondered, didn't things like this happen in the place where I lived, was this place truly magical, or was it the wisdom of the people in this place that only made it seem so?

Summer seemed endless that year. I can't tell you how much I changed outside, but inside myself I began to formulate a strength of character and a nature for caring that I hadn't had before. Walking in the woods I found a little squirrel, hurt by a hunter's trap or maybe by another animal. He had one hind paw that was so gnarled he couldn't climb. He let me pick him up and I carried him in my kerchief back to the house. Grandmother helped me clean his little paw and carefully doctor it with Mercurochrome. We put a splint on and a bandage then found a cage in the barn so that we could take care of him until he healed.

The cousins left early so I had time alone with my grandmother. She took me into the root cellar and taught me about herbs. She walked in the forest with me and taught me to harvest some of the things that she used as medicine. We took care of the squirrel for almost a month. His leg healed and we took him out into the woods and let him go, but when he had scrambled halfway up an oak he stopped. Looking back in our direction, he chattered away as if to try and thank us for our help.

During my last meeting with Sadie, she shared her hardest memories of the days inside the camp when her fellow captives were beginning to die from scurvy and other illnesses. She wept and I did, too. She asked me not to tell my mother about her, but to try and look at my mother differently, the same way that I had looked at the little wounded squirrel that day in the woods. I promised her that I would try to look at my mother through those same eyes. She hugged me tight to her and as I was walking down the path, she called, "Leah, be your mother's memory."

Riding home to Elgin on the train, I thought about how I had changed. I was beginning to feel like a grownup. I knew that when I saw my mother at the station I would be able to do what Sadie asked. I knew too that I would always have the wisdom that she had shared with me that summer. I knew that no matter what happened in my life I would have the strength to bear it without faltering, that I would be a survivor with the strength and courage of the eagle and the ability to give to others with understanding and love.

I Am My Mother's Memory 47

☙ Chapter VI

There they were, my father and my mother, standing arm in arm, watching for me to emerge from the crowd getting off the train. I hung back, steeling myself for the moment and taking advantage of them having not seen me gave me time to really view how they were when I was not in the picture.

Finally, I was nearly the last passenger in my car and the old coachman asked, "Anything wrong, Miss?" I answered hesitantly, "No, sir, I was just watching my folks." He smiled and touched his cap with his hand. "I know how that feels . . . ," he said and he was gone on down the aisle, leaving me to the last moments of my awareness.

It seemed that time stood still for a few moments and then suddenly sped up like a car racing to its destination. I came to myself standing at the edge of the platform, hearing my father's voice. "Over here, my love, over here," he called out. I was in motion, then moving toward them and they toward me. Again I was struck with how very beautiful my mother was and how handsome my father looked in his Irish sweater with the bright cravat in the neck.

There was a quick exchange of hello's and how are you's,

and we were at the baggage pickup getting the suitcases. I felt older than when I had gone away in the early summer. My long, curly hair was pulled up in the back and swung loose over a bright bone comb that my grandmother had bought for me. Mother eyed it carefully and even reached up and gave it a little boost. "Nice," she said.

My father was headed toward the car now with both suitcases and my personal bag in his great hands. Mother and I followed silently. Father, as always, got right to things. As we drove home he filled me in on the progress at the house where he was adding a glass breakfast room, and I filled him in on the way things were this summer at the lake, how the neighbor's boy had died, the place that I went to sit and think out on the great rocks overlooking the river and how I'd seen the Eagle there . . . he gave me a long look when I told him about Ella. "Funny," he finally said. "She gave me a name one day too . . . She called me 'Eagle Flyer,' that's why my plane was named that during the war." I recall a picture of Father standing next to his Navy plane and the wings of an eagle painted on the side and the words "Eagle Flyer" underneath. It felt good to be home when we pulled up the driveway.

I went immediately to my room to unpack. I was shocked when I opened the door: My entire room had been redone — instead of having the look of a little girl's room it now looked like a sophisticated lady should live in it. I set my bags down and walked around, looking things over. My canopy bed had been replaced by a clean-cut Danish modern which had a bookcase in the headboard. The flowery wallpaper was now a tumbling fleur-de-lis pattern in bright shades of maroon and orchid with green stripes. My dresser matched the bed, and so did the side tables on either side of the bed. The doors to the playroom were open and inside were more surprises: a desk with a matching chair, a small couch in a pattern that matched the wall paper in my bedroom. A teacart and a big wing chair finished the set. The only thing in either room that I recognized was my doll that sat on the self at the top of my bed.

I hadn't heard Father and so I was startled to turn and find him standing in the door between my bedroom and the play room. "I hope you like the changes," he spoke softly. "Your mother did it to surprise you; your grandmother said that you were really growing up when she wrote to tell us which train you would be on." "It's all right," I replied. "Did she keep my things?" Father crossed to the nurse's door and opened it wide. "I put them in here. You can save whatever you want." He smiled and patted me on the shoulder as he passed and left me standing there, wondering where to begin.

Normally change didn't bother me, but to come home to a totally different room made me feel sad and somehow a little lost. I told myself that it would be all right once I put some of my old favorite things in among the new stuff, but in my heart I wasn't convinced.

At dinner that evening I tried to tell my mother thank you. She wasn't good at hearing things like that and I wasn't sure that she cared. "I wanted the house to look more modern," was her reply.

School would start within a week and I had outgrown all my clothes so the next few days were taken up with shopping which unfortunately also meant fighting with my mother. Things got so bad that by the second day she gave up, walking away and leaving me in the middle of Gottschalk's. I phoned the house and Father came to get me. Next morning I went out with our cook, Mary. She was fun to go with and we quickly found things that suited me, without any quarreling. Bright plaid skirts and fluffy blouses, tidy plain colored sweaters and vests and several pairs of girls' slacks, which later would cause a ruckus in the house because Mother didn't think that proper young ladies wore them. She would be especially furious because one pair was bright red. Ah, life! Mother had old-fashioned beliefs and ideas. When I came down the stairs that Friday dressed in a blue plaid skirt, yellow blouse and dark blue vest, in nylons and shoes with a tiny heel, I thought she was going to have a heart attack and die on the spot. Father saved me by jumping in quick to say how nice I looked, and Mrs. Stein, who had come to share Shabbat dinner, said "Oh, my . . . how you have grown!" Later, on the way to the temple she would reassure me that I looked really nice.

When school started, Father was off to South Africa. I hated to have him go and lingered at the airport until the plane had left the runway. I felt that he worried too because my mother was beginning to act strange again. She even refused to go see him off. When the cook and I arrived back at the house, she was sitting in the dining room at the table, reading, and didn't speak.

Secretly I had planned for weeks what I would do if she started to ignore me. Sadie had taught me to be able to sit in silence and to speak my thoughts if given an opportunity, so I brought a book that I was reading down to the table and sat down next to her and began to read. She stayed there for a long time. Finally she lay down her book. "What is it?" she asked. I began slowly to tell her about the book I was reading. It was *The Diary of Anne Frank*. Sadie had sent for it this summer and had given it to me as a parting gift. My mother listened without saying anything . . . and then a most amazing thing happened.

She unbuttoned her sleeve and rolled it back, laid her arm out on the dark wood of the new table, and pointed with her finger to the tattoo of numbers. "Look!" she said "Look, this is where they tattooed me, we were all only numbers in those days." She pulled her arm away when I tried to touch it but then she grabbed my hand and laid it over the mark. "I hope you never learn the whole truth, it would break your heart . . . you are soft like your Tante Rivka." With that she rose from the table and walked into the hall.

I sat there alone almost until dark. I cried as I thought about how it might have been for her and my aunt that I knew only by name who had been sent back, as my father told me, because she had TB. They sent her to a sanitarium in England where she stayed for two years. Finally, well enough to leave, she went out on the ship *Exodus*, headed for a new life in the new land of Israel.

Sometimes she sent a card or letter to me so I knew that she now ran an orphanage for children in Jerusalem. Mother never talked about her but had often said that I was very much like her.

I decided that day that somehow I would get my mother to share with me. I held no hopes of her being open like Sadie but I did believe that we had at least opened the door that day and I certainly wasn't going to let it go shut again.

I loved school, learning for me was pure pleasure. I excelled in my studies and my music. I had taken piano lessons since I turned seven and could read music like a whiz. Mother always liked to hear me play. That year in my music class the teacher was a Rabbi's wife. She was pretty and modern but she loved the old Yiddish tunes. One day she brought the class a record of a Yiddish band. One of the songs was one that mother hummed all the time. I begged the teacher to teach me to play it. She ordered the sheet music from New York and at lunchtime every day I went to the music room to practice.

I didn't want to practice the piece at home, I planned it as a surprise for my mother. Missing lunch had two benefits: I got to keep the $1.50 and I also began to thin out! At about the same time our school was forming its first swim team. I had never done much in physical education but I could swim like a fish, so I decided to try out. The coach put me on the list right away!

I was so proud. Mother wasn't impressed when I took the permission slip home for her to sign. "Remember," she said, "if your grades fall you'll just have to quit!" Well, my grades never fell so I got to swim with the team. I even was able to keep up my music.

There were always great Christmas performances at schools then. Ours was one exception. My music teacher Mrs. Lowenthal had a great plan. First the choir would perform the regular "Halleujah Chorus" stuff, a couple of young men would do a spoof on the Every Brothers singing "Rudolph," then I would play "Hativka"!

Mother kept asking why I wanted her to come to the performance, but I held out, it was my secret . . . a gift, one might say, especially for her. Long before the night came I asked Mother to go shopping with me for a dress, a long dress. "Why long?" she queried. "Just because the teacher said so," was my answer. We searched and searched. Mother was patient with me, which surprised me. The search finally ended in Motell's when I found a beautiful navy blue satin gown with long sleeves, little cuffs and collar of cream-colored lace.

When I stepped out of the dressing room, my mother's eyes got wide. She came over and gathered my heavy curls in her two hands, pushing them up into a bunch on the top of my head. "There, like this . . . and you can borrow my pearl combs." It was a grand, wonderful moment! It was the first time that she had ever done anything like that. I wanted to turn around and hug her but I was afraid it would spoil the moment so I didn't. Even now, writing this, I wish I had been brave and tried!

Finally the night arrived. I had asked Mrs. Stein and Mary to go with us, and Mother seemed glad for the company. I left them in their seats and went upstairs to the music room to practice once more. It took forever for all of the wonderful music and the short play by the drama department, then it was the vocal department's turn. My hands shook and my voice trembled as the last notes of "Rudolph" slipped away. The choir sat in their seats on the stage, the grand piano was rolled out from behind the curtain, Mrs. Lowenthal stepped up to the microphone, and her sweet voice rang through the now silent hall . . . We had taken great pains to keep the secret, on the program it merely said:

A VERY SPECIAL PIECE . . . . To Be Announced.

My best friend Carolyn held my hand while Mrs. Lowenthal spoke: "The staff of Cleveland Middle School have decided that we should add a tradition to our Christmas Program. This next piece is for all of those in our audience of the Jewish tradition, and it will be played by my student, Leah Kommarovski-McRyan. She has asked that I dedicate it to her mother."

I felt as if I were moving in a dream. My skirt rustled as I walked out and took my place at the piano. I kept my eyes riveted to the music, I breathed in time to the rhythm of my fingers, and when I ended the piece, at first there was silence and then suddenly a sound of a thousand seats as people stood up, clapping. At first I couldn't move from the bench; there was Mrs. Lowenthal, her hand reached out toward me, I took it and rose, as the room again shook with applause. I couldn't see much beyond the footlights but suddenly there was my mother coming up the steps, behind her several other women who I knew were Jewish. "Again!" someone shouted. I looked hesitantly at Mrs. Lowenthal whose husband now stood next to her. "Again," she whispered. As quickly as that, there was silence as I seated myself at the piano. When I looked up all the lights in the house were on, the choir rose to their feet, I began to play, and the voices of the choir echoed the words. Over the choir I could hear the most lovely voice. At first I didn't recognize it, I thought it was Mrs. Lowenthal's, but then the voice was right beside me, and the words were Yiddish. My mother had never sung loud enough for me to hear her, but the deep resonant soprano was she!

That night was a landmark for Cleveland Middle School: They would, ever after that, use songs and music of other traditions in their programs. The newspaper next day had an article in it about how brave Mrs. Lowenthal and I were to do such a thing and how wonderfully well received it was by most of the audience. But the newspaper also had a letter from a Church of Christ pastor who said that it should never have been allowed, that we had defamed Christmas with our blasphemous behavior.

My mother cried all the way home the evening of the concert, but she kept saying, "It is all right, they are good tears!" We had cake and tea with Mrs. Stein and Mary, then I went up to my room to climb into bed, exhausted by the experience. My mother came and stood in my doorway for a long while. She didn't say anything; she just stood there. I fell asleep with her image still in my mind and her sweet voice in my ear.

The newspaper article by the pastor put my mother in a terrible state; she shook visibly when she read it. I rang up Mrs. Stein and she came right away. They sat together for hours that Saturday, speaking in low, hushed tones. Mother took to her bed in the afternoon and didn't come down to dinner.

Mrs. Stein stayed and tried to help me understand that Mother was affected by the pastor's article. I had a hard time understanding how something could be so lovely and be taken as ugly and wrong!

On Monday in the hall before first class, some boys passed me and called me a kike. When I got to the music room third period, I asked Mrs. Lowenthal what that meant. She explained that some people had not approved of what we had done but that the principal had given his permission and that was all we had needed.

I learned about hatred and bias the hard way that year. People who had been friends suddenly drifted away, others who hadn't even spoken before suddenly thought of me as a hero, and when my relay swim team beat everyone else in competition because of my time I learned that some people only care for you because of what you can do!

My mother didn't seem to be able to get over the fact that the press had published the pastor's letter. She felt threatened and was afraid to go out of our house alone. Father wrote from South Africa that he wanted us to join him there and Mother for the first time said yes.

We arrived in Elizabeth Port by Navy transport plane. I had been fine but Mother was airsick the whole way. The culture shock of our new surroundings sat in immediately. Mary, our cook at home, was black. Here the black people had to walk in the street with the cars and animals; they were not even allowed on the sidewalk. The smells and sounds were so foreign, the way of life so different. Mother loved the house that we lived in as it was a grand old leftover from the days of British rule. She took the embassy by storm. The ambassador at the time had no wife, and state dinners or other such affairs had been sorely lacking.

In no time at all Mother started seeing to things and everyone seemed to love her. I loved being in a foreign land and set about at once to discover as much as I could of this place where we now lived.

Chapter VII

This was not my first experience in a foreign country with my stepfather, but this time I was old enough to pay attention and to understand the injustice that I would witness there. We lived several kilometers from Elizabeth Port in a compound that had been built by the English. It was at once elegant and austere. The rooms were ample in size and well appointed with furnishings dating back to the grander times of sovereign rule. There were servants who were all black, two maids, a cook and two yard boys one of whom was close to my own age.

The compound had a stone wall, which I guess was put up to either keep out wild animals or protect the original inhabitants from the "natives." One was not allowed to communicate with the blacks as they were "uncivilized." I took no heed of that stern warning given to me by the secretary at the embassy, where Father worked. One also was not to become "friendly" with any of the "blacks" as that was a sign of being "uncultured," so right away I was going to be in trouble. Mother had great rules to which I could never aspire, but these rules to me seemed absurd, even ludicrous, for after all the country belonged to the natives; who were we to try to push them out? My first big mistake took place less than three days into our stay. I was out in the compound, sitting by a lily pond, which at the time was not a very pretty sight, and in my own stubborn way of not obeying rules I began a conversation with Samha, the yard boy, who was trying to pull leaves and debris from the pond. My mother spied me from the window and sent the cook to fetch me inside. "Under no circumstance are you to speak to any of the black people while we are here!" she scowled at me as the stern words flew. Then my mouth got the better of me: "Why, Mother, Why? If they are hurt you know the blood is still red, they are human just like us, and you of all people should not show such ignorance and prejudice."

For the second time she struck me in the face. The slap resounded in the hollowness of the high ceiling of the room. I stood stunned, but my mouth would not give in. "You lived through hatred so great that it nearly destroyed all of our people; how can you defend the stupid rules they have here?" She reached out to slap me again but her hand fell short . . . She turned without speaking and walked away from me.

When Father came home that evening I had a long discussion with him. He shared the whys and wherefores behind the rules, which had been in effect since the colonization of the continent by European nations, and spent several hours trying to help me understand. But in the end of things he could see that I just didn't see a purpose in it all, so he said "What do you think should happen?"

I went on and on about my belief that all humankind should be treated fairly, with human understanding, and how I thought that it was wrong to mistreat the American Indian and I also felt that this treatment of the blacks was wrong, especially being that this had been their home long before colonization. Father listened intently, his two great hands pushing against each other, his lips pushed into his index fingers until they were white. "Right!" he finally said. "Right, you are! I shouldn't be surprised if you get us thrown right out of here!" he stated. "But you are right, they are human and some of them are very educated. I guess that I had forgotten some of the things I believe . . . things your grandmother taught me about fairness and rights . . . guess you had to come down here and remind me. Well . . ." There was a long pause. ". . . Listen, let's do this; you try not to let your mother or any of the embassy people see you visiting with the natives and I'll try to help people understand that they are human too."

There it was done, Father and I had an agreement; tomorrow I would go out of the compound and then I could speak with whomever I wanted as long as I didn't get caught! If my mother had known that I told Father about her slapping me I think she would have taken me straight back to the States, but I knew he hadn't said anything to her when she came to breakfast on the verandah, looking as if nothing had happened.

Our six months there flew by. I saw water buffalo in the great river, watched as a herd of elephants marched past the compound, heard lions roar in the night and monkeys chatter in the trees. I even had a spider monkey who adopted me. She came every evening to my window to eat cookies on my desk. Once a huge snake got into my room and made himself at home in the mosquito netting which hung over my bed. I woke during the night to find that he was sinking slowly down toward me. I ran into the yard in my nightgown, screaming wildly, making such a commotion that I woke the entire compound. Two yard boys went and wrapped the snake in the net and took it away. "They'll probably eat it," my mother said flatly.

"They'll sell it to a poacher for good money," my father said. "It will end up in a zoo somewhere in the world or stuffed in some safari collection." I felt bad that I had screamed but the next day Samha told me that the snake was the type that would have curled himself around me and strangled me to death. He said I was lucky that the noise of the netting had wakened me.

I made lots of friends among the native people. They were kind and caring. They had many ways that at first glance might seem strange, but they were much like the Indians I knew on the reservation near my grandmother's — simple people who lived with the land, not from it. I got a terrible sunburn, I fell asleep in the hammock in the yard and woke hours later toasted.

My mother thought I should be whipped but Father took me to the infirmary and I was given something for the pain but the burn itself they did nothing for. Next day I snuck out of the compound and went to visit Samha's grandmother. She lived in the village about two kilometers north. When she saw me she laughed, but she knew it hurt . . . she caught herself. "Do you know what to do for this?" I asked, knowing that she had remedies just like my own grandmother. "Me, able to make burn go away and fix so you never burn no more." She stated, "Come by me, we fix."

She took me to the edge of the river where they had a small dam. First she had me bathe with the liquid she squeezed from a large bag of leaves, then she poulticed me with mud until the pain was gone. I have never had another bad sunburn in my entire life. And yes I was stupid enough to fall asleep while lying in the sun. My burn never did peel, it turned brown. My mother kept saying that I had ruined my skin for life with all the sun but I felt confident that it was not true.

We were often invited to events and functions at other embassies. We were invited to the English Embassy for tea, as it was the Queen's birthday. I was seated with my mother and father but as soon as they got up to go visit with others, I seized the chance to get away with some of the other young people who where there. One English boy in particular interested me. His name was Alistair Kirk. He was fourteen, I was thirteen, and in the embassy schoolroom he and I quite terrorized the poor little English nanny turned teacher for the 39 children of the various embassies there.

I found him sitting with several other boys at a stone table down near the water's edge. He got up right away and came over to meet me. We had gone expeditioning together at times, we had even been to the bazaar *alone*. Our folks either truly didn't know that we often went where we were expressly forbidden to go, or they didn't know how to stop us so they just ignored the issue.

We were both really dressed up that day and uncomfortable as both of us often took to wearing the loose clothes of the natives. We found a place on the grass in the shade and began to share our latest thoughts with each other.

Alistair had recently been north to Kenya with his father who went on a safari. He reported that the natives there really didn't like his father and the other white men, but that they tolerated them as a source of income. He thought this was a good laugh on his father; I agreed. I wanted to know about the safari and he told me that his father had grown disgusted with him and sent him back early because he had no stomach for the killing. I understood! We talked about politics and the way that everyone thought we were better than the natives, and most of all we talked about wanting things to be different. Both of us had friends among the natives who worked in the compound and the embassy grounds; we both liked and respected them for their tolerance of the shoddy treatment they were given by the whites.

Alistair said that he thought Gandhi was right, we needed to learn to live as equals. I hadn't read Gandhi yet but thought I should like to. That day I wrote a note to Father asking if he would buy a book about the Mahatma. It appeared quietly on the nightstand in my room about a week later with a little note inside: "Don't let Mother catch you reading this!"

When we were about to leave South Africa for the States, Father stated over dinner one evening that he had a plan. We were going to fly first to Egypt and then travel overland to Israel so that Mother could see Tante Rivka.

Mother's face went white; she started to say something and then just fainted right into her food. When we finally got her to come around, she wouldn't say anything; in fact she barely talked while we went on for the next three weeks making preparations to return home via the route my father had chosen.

I was very excited. Alistair and I exchanged home addresses and I promised to send postcards from the places we would see along the way. Somehow Father was able to get us a private plane from Durban. The flight to Egypt was long but the benefit was being close enough to the ground to see a lot of the beautiful places in Africa, not to mention the great roaming herds of animals that still were free there. Even though we were on a small plane, Mother was ill the whole way. She said that after this she was not leaving home ever again. And it was "written in stone" because she never did.

Our days in Egypt were wonderful. We saw the pyramids, explored an archeological dig that one of Father's old friends was working on, rode camels, went to the bazaar and had simply a wonderful time. Mother stayed mostly in her room. She said she had no desire to wander around among strange people who smelled bad. The few times that we did persuade her to leave the hotel, she went with a perfumed handkerchief over her nose.

When we finally traveled to Jerusalem to meet my Tante Rivka, Mother was silent the whole way. For three days she never spoke . . . She seemed agitated and afraid, she often threw Father "the look" as he and I called it — it was this glare that she gave when she didn't like something that was going on!

We were in our hotel in Jerusalem nearly a day before the prearranged visit. Mother simply stayed in, "resting," she said, but Father and I went all over. We made lists of what we wanted to see before we were scheduled to leave in two weeks time. The list held all sorts of wonders, the Dome of the Rock, the Way of the Cross, the Knesset building, the Wailing Wall . . . I loved it.

It was a Thursday morning, a bright sunny day with a breeze that smelled like the desert, when we were called to the desk in the lobby. On the way down in the elevator Mother fussed at my choice of clothing. I was wearing a pair of loose-legged khaki slacks and a white sailor's blouse; my hair was loose and brought up on one side with my favorite comb. Getting out of the elevator, I heard my mother catch her breath as if she had been running. There stood the prettiest woman I had ever seen: She had a face shaped like mine and her eyes had a hint of a turn at the corners . . . "Rivka!" Mother held out her arms and they were full instantly.

I had never seen my mother hug anyone, all my life. Whenever she hugged me she just put her right hand on my chest and then sort of squeeze-patted my back. I don't ever recall that she took me in her arms. They were both crying and speaking in torrents of overflowing Yiddish and Russian, when suddenly Rivka broke free, turned and in an instant was hugging the life out of me. I was so shocked. I felt so close to this woman, I hugged right back, and years of never feeling that I was loved by my mother slipped away . . . How could I feel such strong feelings for this person whom I only knew from photos and letters? She cried and held me so close, she put her hand gently under my chin and looked at me as if she was seeing a ghost.

"Leah, my Leah," she said my name over and over.

We went finally into the dining room of the hotel where Father had arranged to have lunch. Tante Rivka sat next to me. She literally moved her chair closer to mine and all through the meal she kept reaching out to touch my hand. She ordered lamb made the traditional way and when our lunch was served she took my plate and divided it. I had a chicken rice dish. She said, "Here we share." So that was my first introduction to flat bread, lamb smothered in onion and garlic, lentils and rice. I loved it, and I found that in my heart I had instantly formed a love for Tante Rivka. The same feeling that I had for my grandmother and Father now sat there like a warm rose-colored stone in my heart. It warmed me just to look at her.

The next two weeks were wonderful beyond description. Father allowed my Tante Rivka to take me to her house to stay with her at night. We loved to walk by the Wailing Wall, holding hands. We learned all about each other. I couldn't stop wondering what it was that made me feel so close to her . . .

We saw everything on our list and then some more. Father arranged day trips to Bethlehem, to Beersheba, Bethsaida — oh how much I loved the country. I never felt so at home anywhere; even my grandmother's slipped to second place behind Israel.

My Tante Rivka was an important person; she ran an orphanage in Jerusalem. The children there were mostly teenagers, some a little younger but most about my age. They were all survivors of the Holocaust. She had started the orphanage with the help of the Government.

She had other ladies who worked there and an English doctor named Silverman who took care of all the medical needs of not only the children there but in five other orphanages in the area. I wondered why Tante Rivka wasn't married and had no children. She was younger than Mother and it seemed strange to me, but I didn't want to pry so I never asked.

When at last our stay drew to a close I was sad beyond expression; the day we went to the airport was difficult! Tante Rivka and Mother both cried all the way there. I tried hard not to give in to the feelings but once we were cleared through customs and waiting to board the plane I couldn't stand it, I dissolved into my Tante Rivka's arms and she held me tight while we both sobbed our hearts out. Hours later on the plane I fell asleep sitting next to my father, still sobbing.

I had a dream that night that Tante Rivka was my mother. I never told anyone about it as I thought that it was silly, but it certainly seemed possible that the love we had for one another was that of a mother and a child. Whenever I was hurt or sad after that I tried to think about the dream . . . it helped me deal with Mother and it made me feel safe.

⇝ Chapter VIII

When we arrived back in the States, I immediately went off to be with my grandmother at the lake. Father had decided that we should find a home in California that would be permanent. He and Mother flew to Los Angeles several days after I left for the lake. I really didn't care if we moved again, as no matter where we were the house without Father was cold and lonely.

Grandmother, as always, seemed not to have changed at all; she was still the Fairy from the pages of my storybook. Her long hair now had a trace of white here and there, but that served to make her seem even more magical than before.

She met me at the train with my uncle Lloyd. She just gasped when she saw me. "Look how tall you are, how much you've changed!" she exclaimed. She made me twirl around right there on the spot to "check on the *real* girl," as she put it. I assured her that the real girl had not changed. She was satisfied with my answer and a tight hug . . . "Oh, you finally learned about hugging!" she looked at me in that deep way that only she had.

When we arrived at the lake, both Spot and Blackie came to greet me — two great dogs, tails wagging, so excited to see me. It felt wonderful to be here again; in my mind often I thought of this as My Home . . . it was after all the first house I had ever lived in.

Much like Grandmother, the house never seemed to age; it always looked as it did the first time I saw it. But little did I know what was coming during this visit or how it would affect us all.

There were no longer any clothes in the old trunk that would fit a teenage girl, so Grandmother took me into the dells and we bought a couple of pair of blue jeans and two shirts. Because Mother no longer packed my bags I had brought some of my favorite things from home, including some of the loose-fitting African clothes I'd learned to love.

The first weekend there I was out in the boat on the lake, fishing, and it suddenly began to turn very windy and cool. I heard Grandmother ringing the great old dinner bell that hung by the porch. Quickly I rowed myself to the shore. Grandmother was waiting there for me with the dogs in tow. "Hurry, Leah," she shouted, "run for the storm cellar!"

When we were safe in the enclosure with the big doors secured, she explained that a tornado was coming. About that time a sound like a thousand trains deafened us. The noise was mingled with the sound of things breaking. Wood slammed against the doors, and the light that hung from the ceiling swung around and went out. In the darkness I clung to Grandmother and she to me while the two dogs huddled at our feet, trembling in fear.

The wind died down after what seemed forever. I let go of Grandmother and started to head toward the door. "No, not yet, it's . . ." But before Grandmother could get the words out the roar of the mighty wind came again; this time it seemed that the doors would be torn away. They rattled so hard that earth from the ceiling fell on us. After the roar died down there was a continuous pounding sound that continued for a long time. We stayed huddled together with the dogs, waiting for the noise to stop.

When finally it grew quiet, we had to force the doors open. It took all of our weight together pushing against them to finally get one open enough to climb out. What we saw stopped us where we were!

Where once the barn stood, there was nothing left but the floor. There were trees torn right out, lying on the ground with their roots exposed. Debris was everywhere. When we finally had the nerve we climbed the rest of the way out and turned to see that the house, miraculously, still stood on its foundation.

Some of the windows were shattered; there were pieces torn out of the roof, but she was still there. Grandmother sank to her knees and began to thank the gods of the wind for sparing the house. I began to recite the Shema. Suddenly our eyes locked and we both started to cry. After a few moments, Grandmother began to wipe her face on her apron . . . "That's enough tears, we've got a lot of work to do before nightfall," she stated matter-of-factly.

So we got right to it, as my father would say. We decided to tend the animals first and make sure that they were okay. The rabbitry was totally a shambles, but as we counted, all eighteen of the breeding doe rabbits were there sitting under the rubble, huddled together. I found six or seven of the boxes that had made up the nests and we managed to tuck all of the rabbits safely into them and secure them with some chicken wire.

Next we tackled the hen house. What a mess! Feathers, broken eggs, hay everywhere. The roof and two of the walls were still intact but somehow the whole front and back had blown away. We couldn't find many of the hens, but Grandmother said that if they were still alive they would find their way back home. I watched as Grandmother handled each hen that remained, her hands running over them under the wings and down the legs. "Here," she said, "take this one and put her in a box so she can't move too much. Her leg is broken." One by one we tended all the animals. It was beginning to get dark before we went into the house. Grandmother had two lanterns from the storm shed so we had kerosene light to see by. The house inside was pretty bad, with glass everywhere, and as I was sweeping up I found dead birds and several squirrels in the rubble. "Bury them tomorrow," grandmother told me.

We weren't able to do much for the upstairs, it was too dark and we were just exhausted. We dragged pieces of wood from the rubble outside and covered some of the downstairs windows. As we were finishing the last one we saw some lights coming up the road. It was a group of men from the reservation. They told us that the storm had torn a path from town straight out to our place; they insisted that we bring the dogs and come to the reservation until morning. Grandmother and I agreed that it seemed the best plan.

We were given a truly royal treatment by our friends, a good meal of venison stew, corn bread, and warm coffee. We slept at Ella's that night in a great bed of warm homespun blankets.

The repairs on the house took up most of the summer. We were able to get most everything back to its original form, except the front door; the pretty piece of leaded glass had shattered. Grandmother bought a piece of plain glass and had it put in. I cried when I first saw it, and I was determined that somehow grandmother would have her door back. Before I went to bed that night I sketched the window in my diary the way I remembered it.

Father cut short his trip in California to return to help us. The summer went quickly with all the work we had to do, but I still had time to steal out to my favorite rock from time to time and sit there, thinking about how life is. There are lots of different storms in life, I decided, some that devastated things and some that devastate lives. I catalogued the Holocaust in the storms that devastate lives.

Some of our animals did find their way back: several ducks, some of the chickens, and the old gray goose, though it would have pleased me if he hadn't. I was working in the barn helping Father to finish the grain bin when I heard him honking. I looked up to see him waddle into the barn. As soon as he spied me the wings shot up and he flew at me. He and I had a long-standing personal dislike for each other; he adored chasing me, and, even at fourteen, I was terrified of him. I dove for the ladder to the loft and climbed up out of reach while my father fell on the floor, rolling with laughter.

Things slowly got back to normal. There was a great swatch through the pines down to the lake where the storm had wiped out hundred-year-old pines and oaks as if they were toothpicks. Grandmother had a huge woodpile that year. She saved every bit of the wood. "If G-d was kind enough to leave them then I should at least make use of them," she said.

Father left the first of August, giving me no hint as to where I would be living come September. He boarded a plane in Madison bound for California. All I knew for certain was that the house in Elgin had sold at "a great profit."

Grandmother and I continued to work on the house. It got better right along. We took time out to visit Sadie and she was very happy to see me. We spent an afternoon catching up on everything that had happened and when we left she gave me an album with pictures from the lectures that she gave.

I went fishing when I had time and had learned the art of casting a fly from my uncle Lloyd so I practiced a lot. I had never caught a trout until one evening, just as the sun began to set, I had walked far up the river toward the reservation and found a clear pool surrounded by rocks. I had been there casting for a while when suddenly he struck. A great German brown trout hit my fly and held on. When I pulled him in and plucked him out of the water in the net, he was so beautiful. The fly was just caught in his upper lip, his eyes looked frightened to me, I could feel his heart beating. Carefully, so as to not hurt him further, I dislodged the hook and let him slip back into the water. He was too wonderful to kill.

I told my grandmother about it over dinner. She smiled at me in her special way. "You're a good spirit," she told me. "It's a grand thing to recognize the value in life. Whether it's a human or an animal, the Indians believe that if you see the spirit of the animal and see his fear that you must not kill him. They believe that to give an animal back his life is a blessing."

I went to bed full of myself that night. I felt good, I felt proud of what I had chosen to do. Next morning I wrote in my diary: "Choice is the important thing. If given an opportunity to choose, one must always consider life!"

I left that summer not knowing where I would be living, only that I had been sent air fare to Los Angeles where a quick note written by Father told me that he and Mother would meet me.

Los Angeles was a real pretty place, with lots of hustle and bustle and full of tall buildings that had a way of jutting around among lots of smaller ones. The plane flew over desert and mountains, and I wondered, where in all that I could see had Father found a place?

It turned out that he had picked a place on the highway between Los Angeles and Palm Springs near Beaumont. It was a ranch. Long, white fences ran down all sides of the property and a nice white ranch house sat on a hill in the middle of it all . . . I loved it! Mother hated it. She complained that it was hours from everything, and who would want to work for us? Father hired a cook and her husband became our foreman. Annie would be with Father and Mother to the end of both their lives, then she would be with me . . . until she died years later. One never finds that kind of loyalty anymore.

Father took an assignment at the English consulate in Los Angeles, but not for long. During the first month in our new home he was reassigned to Paris. I took immediate action, I wrote Father a long note telling him that I preferred not to stay here with Mother, that I wanted to go with him.

I laid it in the middle of his old oak desk and sat his pipe stand on top of it to make sure that he would notice. I had been in bed, reading for almost two hours, when he arrived home. I heard him in his office downstairs and waited. After a while there came a tap on the door. When I answered, he entered, looking stern. "Why ever would you want to come live in an embassy?" he asked. Not one to talk around the bush, Father always struck at the heart of the issue no matter how difficult that seemed.

I told him how Mother and I never communicated, how I

hated silence, how hard it was for me to have no one to share things with and how most of all I felt she didn't care for me, which made me struggle every time he left us. I had thought through all I wanted to say and ended with "Papa, please! I'm old enough to go and besides I don't think she is my mother!"

Such a look! My father's face went white . . . "You haven't been into the files in my office, have you?" he asked. Now I really was curious! "No," I answered, but in the back of my mind I was thinking, "No but now I will be."

Father sat in the chair across from my bed and looked as if he was going to faint. "We, your mother and I, we haven't told you the whole truth," he actually stammered . . . My father, who never ever faltered! "There are some things we have never told you, because that is how your mother wanted it. There are things that I can't tell you without breaking a vow I made to her long ago."

My mind was racing, back to the night she had said over and over, "She is not my child." I was quiet, waiting to see what Father would say next . . . Out of my love for him I wished that he would just blurt out whatever it was that needed to be said, but the part of me that knew him best realized that once he gave his word he never went back on it. He sat there in the pose I knew so well, fingers pushing against each other until all his knuckles where white. "I can't tell you what I want, I must talk with your mother . . . maybe tomorrow . . . Don't think badly of me, try to understand that I cannot let your mother down. I'm really all she has in the world to hold on to."

With that he rose from the chair, came to the edge of the bed, and kissed the top of my forehead. "Goodnight, my little love." He whispered and was gone, door closing behind him as if it were in a soundless void.

I sat there for hours. A part of me knew what he had wanted to say: I am not my mother's child. And the other part began a cacophony of thoughts that would torture me till morning. I had by now gained enough insight into the holocaust to know that some really unthinkable experiments had gone on, and that it was possible that I could be the result of one of those, or that I could be the illegitimate offspring of one of the Nazi soldiers who had been a guard a the camps. The night was not kind to me.

When the sun finally crept through my lace curtains, I got up and went into the bathroom and I took a long hot shower. Maybe I didn't want to know, I told myself; maybe it would have been better if I hadn't pressed Father so for information. Maybe . . . I caught a glimpse of myself in the mirror as I was toweling my hair dry. Suddenly I was looking at a familiar face . . . a pretty face, but a face that I didn't feel comfortable with.

It was still early when I went down to the kitchen but there was always a fresh pot of coffee on in case Father wanted it. I poured myself a cup and walked out onto the back deck. The sun had just peeked up over the mountains and the sky was a beautiful rose color. I sat my cup on the banister, covered my face with both hands, and sang the Shema . . . the way my Tante Rivka did every morning, standing on the roof of her small home in Jerusalem. As I did so, I felt the tears wash down the inside of my hands. When the last words left my lips I picked up my cup and started to walk toward the pasture. The air was fresh, the pink hues of sunrise touched everything with a rosy wash. I had learned to love this time of day while in Jerusalem with my Tante Rivka. I wished that I could fly to her this instant and demand the *truth*! I could see her face in my mind's eye. Suddenly a bright light literally tore through my mind. The face in the mirror this morning was me, but the memory was of her: Tante Rivka, my dearly loved, wonderful, caring, unselfish, aunt. Could it be, was it possible?

I walked slowly, as if in a fog while my mind raced through the known facts, trying to piece together the unknown to make it fit. I don't know how long I walked about but when I came to myself I was far from the house in the pasture where the horses grazed, sitting on the top rail of the fence.

I hadn't heard Father coming but there he was . . . "Are you all right?" he asked.

"Fine," I answered. We walked back to the house while he

explained that mother would not agree to allow him to tell me. I listened politely and before I could stop myself I said simply. "It's all right, Papa, I figured it out . . . I must belong to Tante Rivka!" Father stopped in his tracks; he just looked at me, not saying anything! After a minute or two he simply started to walk on toward the house. When we reached the kitchen door he turned . . . "Don't speak of this to your mother! I will make arrangements to take you with me to France."

Done, just like that, without telling me anything, he told me everything . . . and in the bargain he assured me safe passage away from Mother.

☙ Chapter IX

During the ensuing weeks while getting ready to go with Father, I attended a small private high school in Yucaipa close by our home. Here once again I would learn the pain that ignorance can inflict. I took a letter from my father to the office. In it he said that we would soon be leaving and that he should like a schedule of the classes that I would need to have if ever I was to come back to high school in the States. The heavy-set lady who served as secretary in the school opened the letter on the spot even though it was directed to the principal. "Look here," she announced to the rest of the staff in the office, "little miss prissy is going with her father to France. Who does he think he is? He can't just take her out of school, how's she going to get her education?"

"Excuse me," I tried to be polite. "Excuse me but that letter was intended for the principal." The secretary glared at me, turned on the intercom and announced. "Mr. Daniels to the front office, please." Satisfied, I sat down to wait. When Mr. Daniels appeared, he looked stern. "What's the problem?" he asked. The secretary merely handed him the letter with the torn open envelope, then motioned toward me with her head.

Well, I had no idea that going out of the country could cause such a ruckus. I'd been in and out of the country all my life, but I guess to the folks there it was most unusual. Mr. Daniels took me to his office and sat me in front of his great old desk, "Now tell me, does your mother know about this?"

I bristled. "Yes, sir," I said as calmly as I could. "Are your folks getting divorced?" he asked. "No, sir, my father is an ambassadorial adjutant. We travel all the time, this time I'm going alone with him because Mother didn't like flying when we came back from South Africa."

The principal just glared. Then he said, "A likely story, I shall have to call a conference with your parents to get the truth of this. Go to class and don't tell such wild tales, people don't like liars!"

I wanted to protest but I thought better of it and took myself off to class. During sixth period that afternoon a monitor appeared and handed the teacher a note, one of those pink slips they used to send for you when the principal wanted you. When the teacher called me to her desk she said, "Take your things. You won't be back before class is over."

I trembled all the way down the empty halls to the office. When I walked in, the secretary who had earlier been so rude motioned me to the principal's office. The door was open.

When I entered the room the principal nearly sprang to his feet. "Ah, I'm sorry about this morning," he stammered. My father and mother were seated in front of his desk. "It appears that you are telling the truth so we will be issuing a curriculum for you to take with you on your trip."

Father and Mother stood up, Father shook the principal's hand, and Mother gave him "the look." Father asked me to go get all my things from the locker and meet them in the parking lot. I felt a little sad that I would leave this way; I did enjoy my teachers and had a friend or two whom I would have liked to say good-bye to. Later, on the way home Father said that he was so infuriated with the way the principal had done things that he decided I would leave immediately even though we weren't flying out until the following week.

Mother added that she needed time to get me extra clothes, and besides I needed a physical before we left. The week flew by, I got my boosters for the overseas inoculation requirements and my physical. Mother and I went to Los Angeles three days in a row and shopped until I was near exhaustion. Surprisingly she never asked me why I had asked to go with Father, in fact she never even mentioned it. She was very gracious about what I liked and allowed me deference on almost all of the items of clothing. The only thing she frowned about was a pair of navy blue and white opera pumps. She thought they were too old-looking and I ended up with flat patent leather as usual.

When finally the day arrived for our departure, Mother rode with Father and me to the airport in a government car. She hardly spoke. When we were about to board the plane I went over and tried to give her a hug, which as always she stymied, putting one hand on my shoulder to hold me away while she patted my back. I persisted and managed to plop a kiss on her cheek before she could stop me. "Really!" she exclaimed. I didn't watch as Father said his goodbye but went on ahead and found our seats in the plane.

We flew from Los Angeles to New York where Father had planned a two-day layover so we could visit his sister Sybil and her husband Brad. We stayed at their apartment and went to see *Annie Get Your Gun* on Broadway. I loved it. It was the most fun I had ever had. Afterwards we got to go where some of the cast went to eat because Uncle Brad was a newspaper writer, one who wrote for the entertainment section of the paper. It was terrific, I got autographs from lots of the people in the show on my program. We left New York on a Wednesday morning, stopped in London to see one of Dad's wartime buddies and with his family. We toured London and as usual I got into a bit of trouble. The trolleys moved real fast. I was used to a much slower pace and was looking at the Palace gate and nearly stepped in front of an oncoming bus! A nice young man grabbed me, yanking me back on to the curb just in the nick of time. Dad had planned this stopover because his friend had two girls my age and London was not far from France, which meant we could go over to visit when we had holiday weekends. It was a good plan.

Molly and I were friends right off. She had the brightest copper-red hair I'd ever seen. I told her about seeing Ethel Merman in *Annie Get Your Gun*, showing her my program with all the autographs, and we were off to a friendship that would last a good long while.

We arrived in Paris on a Sunday morning very early. As we were being driven to the house the church bells of the city began to ring; such a sound . . . I was thrilled to be living somewhere with so many beautiful bells. The apartment we would live in had been picked for us by an embassy envoy. When we arrived in front of the building I was stunned. It was so elaborate — old bricks with moss growing on them and lots of decorative trim. There was a doorman like in a big hotel. He loaded our luggage onto a cart and took us into an old brass-appointed elevator up to the third floor. The building was divided down the middle and on each side of each floor there was one apartment.

I followed the doorman in as he opened two great oak doors with carved designs on them. The first thing I laid eyes on was a grand piano! It was lovely, and it sat so that whoever was playing could look out on the street below. The window faced toward the Arc de Triomphe. It was beyond belief.

My room had a bed built into a cupboard. It was such fun. There were curtains and you could pull them around at night and be snug as a bug in a rug. We had maid service and a cook who loved children. She immediately began to teach me things in the kitchen: how to make crepes, how to poach an egg in a pan of boiling water, how to steam vegetables so that they stayed crisp.

I went to school just round the corner from the apartment, close enough to walk. It was a Catholic girls' school, which Father had picked instead of the embassy school as he felt the teachers would be much better. They were . . . should I say, tough, or just plain rigid! I loved going to school and here it was a challenge; at home I always had all the answers, in fact sometimes I knew more about things than my teacher, especially when it came to things like geography or social studies. But at St. Martin it was different. I worked very hard in my studies. In addition to six regular study classes I enrolled in voice and piano courses. My teacher in the piano course was named Wilhelm von Weber. He really didn't like me. At times I could feel his distaste but I hadn't a clue why he behaved that way. I was determined to win him over so I went to a music store and asked if they could get me a copy of a really wonderful German piano piece. They got me Johannes Brahms' Opus 1, 2 & 5. I then had Father purchase me a record so that I could hear the piece. I worked on it for a month until finally I had the magical feel of it down. I took it to piano class and lingered afterward until the other students had gone. I simply asked Mr. Weber if I could play something for him that I was working on at home. "Proceed," was his reply and he sat down at the conductor's platform as was his usual teaching mode. He didn't stir until I had finished, letting the last bar of the andante molto slip away before he rose. Coming over to the piano, he looked down at me over his pince-nez glasses. "That is precisely right, it is as the master wrote it to be played," he said. "Now I give you an assignment, go home and practice it with your heart!" I was at first confused, then I played it for Papa and he said that I needed to read about Brahms so that I could "get the feel" for the piece. Another week passed while I read the life of Brahms, but when I played for Mr. Weber at the end of that week, he actually smiled at me, "Now you are playing with your heart!" He said it kindly and after that he warmed up toward me. I no longer felt he didn't like me but that he enjoyed my playing, and it pleased me.

    Mother wrote to Father weekly, complaining of the house, the area, the distance from "real life" as she put it, and I suppose that Father wrote back. She never directed any mail to me, although I sent out a weekly missive of my activities and my school progress. I did read the letters she sent Father and she did at times say she missed us, but that was all. Father said over dinner one evening that when our leave came we would fly home for forty days to find a place mother liked better, maybe San Francisco, he said. Next day I looked up San Francisco in the encyclopedia in Fathers' study. I wrote a long letter to mother telling her all about how beautiful it was there, about the Golden Gate Bridge and about the style of life there. I don't know if she ever got the letter, but at least I tried.

Father brought a surprise home one night. He had called to simply state he was going to be late, and I had caught a gay note in his voice but wasn't prepared when the door opened and in came my Tante Rivka! I was so thrilled, she had come to visit at Father's request and was to stay for two whole weeks, and I fairly danced around the room.

Father was good at surprises, he had even planned where we would go and what to do and see while she was with us, and he had asked the maid to make up the room next to mine! It was fabulous!

We went to museums, to cathedrals to look at the great windows, and one afternoon we went to see the stained glass being made. I took note of the man's name who did the demonstration for the group we were in; I had a plan to return later with my sketch of my grandmother's front-door window.

We went to synagogue. It was my first time in a while as there were no synagogues close to where we lived in the States. I loved it. Tante Rivka made me remember how good it felt to be with someone you loved dearly. We took walks to see great places and sometimes just so we could talk. In the back of my mind lurked "The Question." One afternoon in the warm sun we walked along the left bank, watching young artists doing sketches and painting. We sat down for a while near the river's edge. In a moment of silence, which was rare with us, I blurted out the story of the night I had shared with my father my feelings about my mother. Tante Rivka sat still as a stone. She didn't blink . . . she looked at me a long while . . . then she reached out with her gloved hand, tipped my face up toward her and asked, "Who do you think your mother is?" Not hesitating, I replied, "You, I think it's you!" Time stood still, it seemed. Suddenly she had her arms about me and there were tears streaming down her face. "I am so sorry, so sorry," she whispered over and over again, "I didn't know that she would not be able to love you! I did what I thought was right, what was best for you, I had to leave you with her, I didn't know what would become of me!"

We sat there in silence, crying, holding on to each other until there were no more tears. I told her that I understood, that it was all right and that I had a good life. She told me how she felt empty when she left me, how her life was turned upside down. She talked to me about why she founded the orphanage and how loving the children who had lost their families made her feel more whole. She explained that she had wanted to tell me when we met the first time in Jerusalem but that Mother had begged her not to. The sun began to set on us before we finished. We walked back to the apartment arm in arm; Father had just come in ahead of us and when he saw us he knew that the truth had finally been told.

We spent the next days walking the streets of Paris, talking about life, hers and mine, and how things happen that all of us just must deal with. I had another question forming in my heart but one I decided that right now, here in this time, I didn't want to ask. So I wrote in my diary: "Today I know that I have a real mother, someone braver than I could ever be, who did something so hard it nearly broke her heart. Most of all someone who loves me without my even trying to please her!" On the next page I wrote: "Do I have a real father, and if I do who is he, where is he?"

Papa was great, he gave us lots of time alone and when Tante Rivka's two weeks were up he told her that he would send me to Israel in the summer if I wanted to go. We went back to the States shortly after that. I didn't mention anything to Mother about Tante Rivka's visit; maybe Father did, I don't know. We were too busy getting Mother a new home in San Francisco to discuss things. We found a place right away that mother loved, high on a hill with a great view. It was on Russian Hill, a corner lot with a weeping willow down at the edge of the lawn near the street. The drive came in from the side so there was a nice front and back yard. The house sat kitty-corner to the street on both sides, and inside it was gorgeous — two stories of drop-dead elegance. I wondered why Mother needed so grand a place when she was usually in it all alone except for the servants. Ann and her husband had nothing keeping them in southern California, so when Father offered an increase in wages and the servants' apartment over the new garage, they took the offer. I was glad because I liked them both and knew that they were used to Mother.

Father got a swift escrow — fifteen days — and had our things brought up while we waited for the closing. It was a whirlwind of activity and I realized that this suited Father since it left little time for anything serious to come up. I could sense that he had not discussed Tante Rivka with Mother, and that he had no intention of doing so.

Mother got in and somewhat settled as our time began to run out. We were all working in the study, putting books on the shelves one day when she seated herself in one of my father's red leather chairs and asked, "Would you take me to get a dog?" I almost fell off the ladder I was working on. We had never had a dog in the house because she would not allow it. Father was as startled as I was, but in his usual fashion he laid down the pile he was working on. "When would you like to go?'" he asked simply. "This afternoon," Mother replied. So it was that we found ourselves in a large pet store. There were a couple of dozen pups, but right off I could tell that Mother liked the collies best. There were two, a male and a female. Cute as they could be, they wagged their whole bodies when they wagged their tails. "Which will you have?" my father queried. Without a moment's hesitation Mother said, "Both." Both it was; Mother named them Freidl and Moshe'. Father ordered a dog run built for them near the garage, but I don't recall that they ever used it. Mother trained those dogs well, they could do every trick in the book, she loved them. She bathed them, groomed them, walked them. And at night, sitting before a fire, they sat on the sofa with her, Freidl with her head in Mother's lap. Father and I never stopped commenting about that!

The forty days came to an end. Mother didn't come with Ann to take us to the airport. I was glad to be going back. France was a good place, I loved the apartment, I even loved the school I went to, and most of all it was close to my Tante Rivka, my real mother!

During the flight back I studied the picture of my grandmother's window. I began to make a bigger sketch of it. I was so intent that Father finally asked what I was working on. I showed him. He admired my drawing and asked if I had a plan for the picture. "Yes," I stated matter-of-factly, "I'm going to see if the glass men at the Window Works can make a new window for Grandmother's front door." Father smiled; he never ever shattered my plans for anything, but I know, looking back, that he surely knew that this would be costly, not to mention the freight to move it from France to the U.S.

Father let me go on drawing, he even supplied the appropriate dimensions. "They will ask you for the size, you know," he stated matter-of-factly.

I fell asleep still working on the picture. In my dream I saw the door of Grandmother's house with the window reflecting the rainbow of sunlight.

Chapter X

Once more we spent time in London with the Macleods. Molly and I wandered all over the city, visiting many of the beautiful old gardens, having just great fun for two teenage girls. Father and the Macleods took us to see the Beatles! They weren't famous yet, we saw them in the pub where they performed regularly. I recall that Molly and I squealed with delight at the music and their antics on the stage. Mrs. Macleod knew Paul McCartney's folks; she got him to sign the napkins we had on our table. He was gorgeous . . . I nearly swooned in my seat when he sat down with us! Molly and I became instant fans.

Molly and I wrote daily back and forth across the channel, talking about the new music, the latest fashion fads . . . and our worry about the things happening in Vietnam. Father and I were both glad to be back in Paris. It was spring and the whole city took on a different look, flowers and trees blossomed everywhere. One Saturday I rode down to the Window Workers. They gave tours all the time so I stood in line for tickets and when I reached the clerk I asked if I could see Monsieur PeLar. The clerk asked what I wanted with him and I explained that I needed to speak with him concerning the making of a very special window.

She hesitated but motioned for another lady to take the tickets and ushered me inside to an office marked "Supervisor." She used a phone to call out to the work area, asking the Mnsr. PeLar to come into the office. Looking back, I don't know why the clerk took me inside to Mnsr. PeLar but she did. Mnsr. PeLar had been working and at first was out of sorts for having been called into the supervisor's office. "Mnsr., the young lady you see here wants to discuss a window with you," the clerk motioned in my direction. I was standing at a window that looked down onto the work floor where dozens of men were busy toiling away at the art of leaded glass making. "Humph!" Mnsr. PeLar groaned but came over to me, "I am a very important glass maker, and I only make windows for great halls and churches, why is it that you want to take up my time?" I remained polite and told him the story of my grandmother's window. Pulling my sketches from my pouch, I laid them out on the table. I had done several more since the one on the flight, attempting to get it perfect. I had used water colors to fill in the colors. At first Mnsr. PeLar just glanced at them, but suddenly he picked up the one I had colored and began to study it in earnest.

"This window, where did your grandmother get it?" he asked. I told him that I really didn't know but that I knew it was the type of work done in this place, that it was called a Rose Window, and that most importantly I had gone on a tour with my Tante Rivka here and seen him working on a window of the same tones. He was impressed. He seated himself at a sketch table with many instruments meant for measuring. He took a long while to figure and measure and refigure. Finally he looked up, "This window, how do you plan to pay for?" I laid out the francs that I had been saving up from my allowance, almost 200 of them. "I know this isn't near enough, but it's a start, I can give you 40 francs a month until it's paid for." Mnsr. PeLar looked as if he would laugh, but he caught himself. "This window, it is very important to your grand mere, no?" he said, looking at me with his dark eyes as though trying to peer through me. "It is *very important* to her, to me, and most important to the house... You see the house is magical . . . well, I mean . . ." My stream of thought trailed off as I tried to think of how I might convince him, but then I noticed that he was smiling, and his whole face was alight with mirth!

"Mademoiselle, I shall make the window." Picking up my 200 francs, Mnsr. PeLar put it together with my sketches and his figuring into a large envelope. "Yes, I shall make the window and you shall help me!"

I didn't want to learn about leaded glass, I was already very busy; but I wanted the window badly, so badly that I said yes! Mnsr. PeLar sat down again, stroking his chin with his hand. One could literally see his mind whirling with thought . . . "This is what we will do: You will come here every other Saturday afternoon precisely at three. We will work with the presentation glass, glass that we make for the tours. I can salvage a great deal and make sure that we get the colors we want by asking the other glass makers to save shards as they work on their projects!" He never did tell me what the window would cost and in my excitement I forgot to ask. Later that evening I went to Father's study to talk with him about the window. At first he seemed hesitant, then he decided that it would be a good experience for me. He said that he would go around and speak with Mnsr. PeLar and make sure that things were set up appropriately. I was very proud and thanked Father with a great hug and kiss on the cheek . . . I turned back at the door to say goodnight but Father had picked up Mother's picture from his desk and was looking at it with a sad expression on his face.

Now my life was very full, school was hard. My courses took a lot of homework and we were responsible for lab times in biology on our own time. My music also turned serious about this time. One day during piano study Mr. Von Weber made a point of keeping me after, "You are becoming a true genius with expressive playing," he said. "I should like you to give a recital." "Alone, like the seniors?" I asked, shaking at the prospect while thrilled that he would think I was that good. "Yes, alone!" he said harshly, "of course alone. What did you think, I was going to have a friend do it with you?" I was used to him now and it didn't frighten me when he went off yelling, it was just his way. "When," I managed to stammer. "In November, with the senior class . . . maybe at the beginning of the season." "Tell your father, see what he says, you can let me know on Monday." I just nodded and walked out into the hall. I couldn't seem to catch my breath, then I realized that I had been holding it. I was so excited!

My father was so pleased, he went right away to talk with Mr. Von Weber. They set a date — November 5 — and Father said that even though I was not in the senior class that Mr. Von Weber felt I should have a dinner after the recital. Father set about dealing with the particulars of that part of the society tradition, while I began to pore over music books to decide what to perform. I very much loved Greig, but my hands were not strong enough for the pieces that he wrote. My next choice was Mendelssohn; I chose "Opus 102," his song without words first published after his death, then his much-celebrated "Spring Song." Next was "Consolation," and I would end my program with the "Scherzo in E minor." Total time would be approximately 45minutes. The study time would run into a little over two hundred hours!

I told everyone; first, Tante Rivka who made immediate plans to come for the occasion; my friend Molly in London, who promised to force her whole family to come; and I called Mother, but she only said, "That's nice, dear." Now my time was divided between homework, practice, and the Window project, as my father started to call it. I loved the smells and the sounds at the glass works. Mnsr. PeLar was a gentle giant of a man whose hands always looked black and seemed never to be without a cut here or there. True to our agreement I did help; it was my personal selection of the shards that we used, which he said would make the right "magic" for the window. So for two hours every other Saturday I would pick through the three great boxes of shards under his old bench. He would tell me which color he needed next and I had to work at the sorting until he said, "Fini, is enough for this piece." He made me work with my back to the table where the iron form that would hold the pieces lay, he never let me peek at what he was doing, not even one little look. The Saturday after I learned that I would give a recital I told him and asked if he would come. "I would be very honored!" he said, bowing to me as if I were royalty. As we worked together, backs facing each other, we talked. He told me about the Second World War and how it had affected him. I shared how my life began and how only recently I had discovered that my real mother was Tante Rivka. On that particular day I learned why he had decided to make my window. He had been married to a Jewish woman, they had three sons . . . he lost them all in the war. They had lived in a small town in Austria then; he worked for a glass factory there. One day he said he went home and his wife and sons were gone, his home in shambles, the door smashed in. Things lay broken everywhere. A neighbor told him how they had been taken. He said he took the things that had meaning for him, packed his bags, and left Austria on foot, walking all the way back to France! He told me that when he saw the little star on the chain round my neck, he wanted to cry . . . it reminded him of his wife. Then when he saw the love I had put into my sketches, and the desire of my heart to give Grandmother back her window, he was totally taken. When I left that day he walked me out to the street, I gave him a little hug! I was learning more than how to pick shards in the right colors, I was learning that you could grow to love people who are not family just because you share their story.

The spring gave way to summer, I was going to Jerusalem for three weeks, and my music would come with me as Tante Rivka said I could practice in the orphanage where they had a piano. I wanted to take more time but I needed to be back for school. I had decided to take classes year round while we remained in Paris.

I worked two Saturdays in a row with Mnsr. PeLar to get enough shards picked to keep him going during my absence. He gave me a small oval-shaped piece to take with me as a gift for Tante Rivka. It had a beautiful Star of David in the center surrounded by what appeared to be rainbows; he said it had all the colors in it that we had picked for Grandmere's window.

Father took me by plane to Jerusalem. He didn't want me to fly alone. I was glad for his company; we always had a good time together. We arrived in the evening and the airport was congested; we were circling longer than it took us to fly from Paris.

Tante Rivka met us. She now had a car, a nice Peugeot. I heard her thanking Father for it later that evening over dinner. We went to the Hotel King David to eat; it was so good. Food in France was always mouth watering, but the food in Israel did more than feed you; it somehow affected your very soul! Father flew back to Paris next morning as he had duties that couldn't wait. I had a moment of hesitation when he was getting ready to board his plane, but he assured me that this would be good for me. Going down the aisle through the gate, he waved merrily, "Remember, little love . . . you are here for a holiday." He often teased me for being too busy to have fun with the rest of the teens of the world.

Tante Rivka and I had a great time. We went to see her friends who lived in a kibbutz. It was great to see how all the parents interacted with all the children as if they all belonged to everyone. I loved the communal feel and the spirit of genuine love that seemed to be everywhere. We stayed for three days then returned to Jerusalem. Tante Rivka loved to have me play the piano. She played the violin like my father and would often get it from the case and play quietly with me. We went for long walks, shopped in the bazaar, visited the Wailing Wall four times, went to the newly established Antiquities Building. It was the first time that I had seen any of the historical side of Israel. I enjoyed learning how the state was formed, how it had been partitioned for us as a people. One gets a different feel for the modern-day country; the historical country is very rich and romantic!

We often spent evenings talking and sharing parts of our lives that were important. I told Tante Rivka how I had worked to make Mr. Von Weber like me. She smiled then explained that he was probably a leftover from the old school of Germans who still didn't care for Jews. I really had never thought of that, but it made his praise of me seem very important. Tante Rivka said that what I had done was a mitzvot, because I had acted lovingly from my innocence and changed his way of viewing me.

We never went to bed without the proper prayers and by the time the three weeks slipped past, I was accustomed to prayer with everything. Right before I was due to leave, Tante Rivka bought me a very special gift. It was a pair of candlesticks and a lovely table cloth of lace. There was a challah cover in dark blue with silver trim and a book of all the blessings. I promised her that I would keep Shabbat when I returned home.

Father flew back to Jerusalem again and we spent three days doing tourist things, then we were off. I cried as I said good-bye to Tante Rivka, but her strong arms held me close and she whispered, "I love you, my child, I will always!" My world felt whole, my tears dried up. I waved to her and called out, "Shalom, Mamaleuchen, Shalom!"

Chapter XI

Summer went by so quickly. It was September before I realized it! Two months left to practice! I was fanatical; every measure of every line had to be perfect before I would let it go. Mr. Von Weber nearly lost patience with me. "Fraulein!" he would shout, his resonant deep voice echoing in the practice room, "From your heart, not from your head!" By the first week of October, I had all the music memorized. "Relax!" said Father. "Again!" shouted Mr. Von Weber. My only relaxation came from my weekly visits with Mnsr. PeLar, who would talk to me about the importance of using your soul to do your work. "In other words, little Mademoiselle, play from your soul," he would urge whenever I brought up the practicing.

Father came to the rescue. One bright October afternoon, we took a plane to London for a short visit with the Macleods. I thought it was strange that Father would suddenly decide on a trip, but there we were in the airport at Heathrow when suddenly, as if by magic appeared my grandmother! I was overjoyed! Father had her come early to be with me for the next little while and to help me see to the all-important dress, he said. But I knew he had brought her over because Mother wouldn't come. It didn't matter, this was wonderful! Mrs. Macleod, Grandmother, Molly, and I looked at every dress in London during the next two days. I finally settled on a demure little silk; it was navy blue with long sleeves, a jewelry neckline and a long bell skirt to make it easier to sit at the piano bench.

For shoes, I finally got a pair of navy opera pumps with short heels. Father was intense; he wanted me to have everything new from the skin out, so I got my first set of colored undies: bra, panties, slip. They all were dark blue. For the first time in my life, I bought colored stockings, also blue!

Right before we were to leave London, Father had the taxi stop at a jewelry store. He went inside and came back with a bag. He didn't say anything, just handed it to me. Inside, there was a velvet and leather box with a gold-hinged closure. "Go on," Grandmother said. "Open it." Inside was the most beautiful set of pearl earrings I had ever seen; where the post went through the ear there was a flower made of blue stone. The center was a bright white pearl. The necklace was made up of pearls and the same dark blue stones interspersed. It was the nicest thing I had ever owned. It made me cry!

Father was delighted; so was Grandmother. Later they told me how they had waited until I picked out the dress and then slipped out to the little jeweler to get the set.

We were back home in Paris in no time; it's a short flight from London. I sat down at the piano immediately, having been remiss with my practice for the past four days. Grandmother went to get settled in one of the guest rooms. She came out right in the middle of "Consolation." She didn't say anything; she walked over and stood behind me, laying her beautiful, tanned hands on my shoulders. Suddenly, my hands trembled and just as they did, the music took wing. I could feel the heart of the piano beating. I relaxed; the music flowed.

Next morning, when I went over to the practice room to play for Mr. Von Weber, he too said nothing. Usually he was wont to stop me several times to correct some error in note or time or phrasing. Not so this time. When I had finished the "Scherzo," he began to clap. "Encore! Encore!" he shouted. I could hardly believe my ears! "Enough now," he said, coming to the bench. "No more practice until the day of the performance. Play whatever you like but not these pieces!" I knew from some of the seniors that he was very stern when it came time for a recital, that some of them where made to come to practice three and four times a day. "But, sir," I started to protest. "No more! Is enough! Is perfect!" "Any more and you will overdo it. You need to rest; go out; visit with your grandmother, but don't play these pieces until the day of the performance!"

I was frightened. What if I forgot? What if my memory slipped? What if? What if? But he was so stern that I went home, put down the music on the piano and went to find Grandmother. When I finished telling her what had transpired, she threw her head back and laughed. "He is right! You have practiced them to death. You play beautifully but you are too worried! Let's go for a walk. You know I have never been to Paris before; this is my first time! Come, show me this world you love so much." So we toured Paris. We went to museums, parks, the Eiffel Tower, the Arc de Triomphe . . . we did them all, and Grandmother loved it. We laughed and ate pastries until I was afraid my dress might not fit! I told her about Tante Rivka. To my surprise, she had known all along. She told me that Father told her years ago, before he married Mother. I felt a little hurt. Grandmother was my best friend; I wondered why she didn't tell me. But when I asked her she simply said, "Your father asked me not to interfere." That told me all I needed to know.

Saturday before my recital, I was due at Mnsr. PeLar's. When I arrived, he said, "Today is special! The window is Fini!" He led me to the work bench, seated me on his tall metal chair and asked me to cover my eyes. My heart whooshed in my ears when he said, "All right!" It took me a minute to take my hands down. There on the bench was the window. It was so beautiful; the colors were so perfect I thought I was dreaming. There was a place at the bottom of the window with a tiny piece of white glass. I leaned forward to see it better. Into the piece, Mnsr. PeLar had inscribed: "M. PeLar & Leah 1962." I grabbed Mnsr. PeLar round the neck and hugged him tight. When I let go, I couldn't help but notice that his eyes shone with tears. "I haven't finished paying you. I don't even know how much I owe . . ." I stammered, trying to regain my own composure.

"Leah," he said, then he handed me the big envelope that he had first placed my sketches and the original money in. "Open it, please," was all he could say. I did. What I saw made the tears sting my eyes. Inside were my sketches, notes he had made along the way, and all of the money I had given him, the first 200 francs and all the payments tied together with a bit of ribbon and a note. It said simply: "Deeds of friendship need no payment!" I hugged him again!

I went straight to the embassy to find Father. He was in his office, alone. I told him that the window was finished and showed him the envelope with its precious contents. Father thought that we should take Grandmother to the Window Works that afternoon. He rang Mnsr. PeLar who said he would be delighted to have us come. We went back to the apartment, ate a quick lunch, and rode over. Grandmother was fascinated by the workers in the exhibit area. She was surprised when Mnsr. PeLar came out from his booth and shook hands with Father. They exchanged a few words in French, then Mnsr. PeLar took me by the hand and motioned for Grandmother to follow. The moment we entered the shop Grandmother cried out, "What have you done, Wilhelm?" thinking, of course, that my father had purchased the window. "Not I," Father answered softly. "But . . ." Now she was looking straight at me. "Leah, you did this? You worked here and did this?" Mnsr. PeLar told our story to Grandmother, careful to leave out that he had given me back all the money this morning. I filled that in for her. She just stood there looking at the window, tears streaming down her face. Finally she turned to face us, great hands folded in front of her. "Will's father bought me the first window. It was to go into a building in the dells and had come from France. When it arrived, it was the wrong size, only about half as big as they had ordered. The town mayor decided to put the window up for auction. I don't know how much he bid, just that he came home with it one afternoon, saying he was going to make me a new front door. We lived in the workmen's house while we were building the main house. I thought it was the most beautiful thing I had ever seen. He had to hire a workman from Madison to make a door to fit the window. I was real upset that it broke in the tornado but I never told anyone!" she turned to Mnsr. PeLar extending her hand. "Thank you," she said quietly, then she grabbed me and hugged me close! "My only Granddaughter," she told Mnsr. PeLar. Father and Mnsr. PeLar made arrangements for the window to be shipped to the States. It would take three months to reach Grandmother. She said that she would get Uncle Lloyd to go to Madison for it.

The next day, the Macleods arrived for their stay with us, as well as Tante Rivka. I was beginning to get very excited. The Macleods were staying at the Anniston Hotel, but Tante Rivka was in the other guest room at our apartment. My days were full of friends and family. Mr. Von Weber had me come to play for him the day before my recital. "Wonderful!" he exclaimed in his deep German manner.

The morning of the recital dawned early. Tante Rivka, Mrs. Macleod, Molly, and myself were off to the hairdressers. I was so nervous that I could hardly sit still in the chair and, once under the dryer, I kept popping out to ask if I was "done" yet. Finally the hairdresser warned, "Mademoiselle, you shall never be 'done' unless you sit still!"

Hair ready, a small but pleasant lunch eaten, it was time to get dressed. Once I had my clothes on, the butterflies in my stomach really took flight. Father smiled. "Formation, my dear. You must get them to fly in formation!" He hooked my necklace for me. I stood a long while looking at myself in the dressing-room mirror. My Tante Rivka and Grandmother came in to see if I needed anything. "Look at you; you look like a young lady!" Grandmother said. Tante Rivka's eyes filled up and nearly brimmed over. "All grown up," she said quietly.

The ride over to the hall where the recital would take place seemed to take forever. The streets of Paris were crowded if you aren't in any hurry to get where you are going, but they were worse if you want to get somewhere quickly! I don't recall how I felt right before taking my place at the piano, but I recall that Mr. Von Weber announced me as "The best young pupil in my class, with exceptional ability to make the music come to life!" Suddenly I was at the piano. My fingers trembled as I struck the first notes. The rest was like a blur. I listened to the music as if it were being played by someone else. When the last notes of the final piece drifted into silence, I rose from the bench to face the audience. To my surprise, they were all standing, clapping loudly with shouts of "Bravo!" and "Encore!" Mr. Von Weber came out and presented me with an arm bouquet of white and red roses tied with a dark blue ribbon. The audience stopped clapping and I seated myself at the piano again. I played Hativka. When I finished, the crowd clapped exuberantly. I curtsied two or three times and left the stage.

My friends and family would meet Father, Tante Rivka, Grandmother, and I at the restaurant near the Arc de Triomphe where Father had arranged for the customary meal. Everyone told me that I had played superbly. I knew I had done really well when Mr. Von Weber told me that he expected I could be a concert pianist if I wanted to. The meal was lovely. There was a chamber orchestra and after we ate, we danced. I felt on top of the world. Father looked proud as a peacock; he danced with me twice then made the rounds with Tante Rivka, Grandmother, Molly, and some of the ladies from the embassy. It was a night to remember for the rest of my life. Mnsr. PeLar danced with me, as did Mr. Von Weber and several of Father's friends and many of the young men from music class and school. Long into the night we partied, even stopping on the way home to have dessert for the second time. I fell into bed that night, exhausted, feeling accomplished while at the same time feeling sad that Mother who had raised me didn't care enough to come. I salved my sadness with the knowledge that everyone whom I loved had been there with me and that it had indeed been grand!

I hadn't gone into the living room the night before, so you can imagine my surprise when I walked in next morning to find literally dozens of bouquets, baskets with fruits and cheese, even one with a bottle of Dom Perignon. Father was just setting down a bright vase of mums. "Ah, I see by your face that you didn't look in here last night. You have lots of admirers," he said. As he passed me on his way out he gave me a little squeeze. "Better look at the cards, but don't take them from the bouquets. You'll need to remember who sent what when you write the thank-you notes."

I walked around and around the room, reading each card over and over. It seemed almost unreal. I didn't know how many people really loved me! There was bouquet from the Ambassador with an invitation to play at the embassy, and a wonderful surprise! There was a crystal vase full of white roses from Mother. There was also a basket from Alistair with a note apologizing for not being able to come but promising that we would see each other soon.

After breakfast, Molly helped me to write down all the names and next to them exactly what they had sent. We went out to the stationers and bought some lovely thank-you cards with tulips on them. Then we set to work. When I finished, the stack of cards numbered forty-two. I was amazed! Slowly, over the next three days, everyone left, until at last it was only Father and I again. Tante Rivka and Grandmother left the same day. Seeing them off, I realized that I loved them both equally, and it appeared that they loved each other too. They hugged each other tightly when it came time for Grandmother to board her plane. I thought to myself how very blessed I was to have such a family. Even for all the secrets, I could still count myself thankful. Being truly wise, I decided, is knowing when to tell the truth and when to let the truth find its own way out.

↦ Chapter XII

  Life resumed a more normal pace. School was now my primary occupation; I loved it! Learning made me feel accomplished. Mr. Von Weber praised me in front of the entire music class for my recital. He said he truly enjoyed working with me and kept stating over and over that if I continued my studies and wanted to, I could become a concert pianist. "At least, be a professor of music," he would say when I told him that Father thought music was not a career or good enough as a profession. I continued to drop by the Window Works to visit Mnsr. PeLar. Often, he would show me his latest creation or some project that he was working on, and ask me to help pick the colors. It pleased me that he still had time for me when I knew how very busy he was.

  Grandmother phoned the day the window arrived in Madison. It had taken a mere five weeks. She was very pleased; the door was all ready and waiting. She said she was going to have a party when the door was put in! I felt lonely, I guess maybe homesick. I hadn't gone to the lake in the summer and I realized that it was the first time in all the years since my folks married.

  Father was due for a change. We had been in Paris almost

eighteen months, and we thought probably around the holidays, we would go home to the States and be there for a while. But fate had other ideas. Father was given a new appointment to Tokyo, Japan, and there would be no time to go home in-between, as the serving Adjutant had to fly home with his ailing wife. We were told that we would transfer on the 15th of December. I was upset as I had planned to be involved in the Holiday Concert at school. But there was nothing to be done. When you are under the employ of the government and they say go, you simply pack. I made the rounds of all my friends. Mnsr. PeLar said he would never forget me, and we promised to find each other again someday.

Mr. Von Weber actually got tears in his eyes. "You are the only young Jewish person I've ever known personally. You are so very talented and smart! I shall look for your name in music news! Be brave, do what your heart wants, not what your father says. I ruined my life because I followed my father's wish and worked for a madman!" He shook my hand solemnly, then at the last moment grabbed me and kissed me firmly on each cheek. "Auf wiedersehen!" he whispered. Looking back when I reached the door, I saw him holding his handkerchief to his eyes.

We sent some things home to Mother and Grandmother, packed what we needed for the five-day leave that we were given and went to Israel. And for that I was very happy! We arrived in the dead center of Chanukkah. I loved the festival of lights, and being with Tante Rivka and the children in the orphanage was great fun! We did no sight-seeing, just took part in the life of the orphanage and enjoyed being with Tante Rivka. Five days flew past in a heartbeat, and we were in the air on our way to Tokyo.

On our arrival at the embassy, we found that we were to be billeted in one of the buildings on the grounds. Father frowned and said in private that we would find a house somewhere outside of the city. Tokyo was not as gracious as Paris had been. The only thing that made it good for me was that Alistair was there too. He and his father didn't live on the embassy grounds but had a nice little house out in the country. Father and I went out to visit him and his family on our second weekend in Tokyo.

They had a wonderful place; it had a wall all around, and the house was made of stone and dark wood. The house went around the garden so that every room opened out into it. It was enchanting!

Alistair and I quickly caught up with our stories and began to get reacquainted. He was much taller than I remembered, and he said that I was thin and also much prettier than when he had seen me last. I blushed! I wasn't used to the compliments of a handsome young man. He was seventeen and finishing his last bit of high school. He thought that he would go back to the States and attend university on the East Coast somewhere, maybe Harvard.

After our visit, Father decided to have our driver take us around the little village. We looked at a few houses that seemed empty and did as Alistair's father had suggested. Father simply got out and went to speak with the nearest neighbor. The country people were very polite. At the second place we stopped, Father was directed to the owner of the house. He actually lived in Tokyo now, so when we arrived back that afternoon, Father phoned up Mr. Woo. He agreed that if we would pay in American dollars, we could rent the pretty little house; he called it the House of the Willows. Next day, we drove back out to the little house, which also had a wall of stone around its gardens. There were indeed great willow trees, four of them in the back and two in the front. The house itself was made in the shape of a U; inside the shape was a pond and a shrine, and across the opening, a great fence of dark red with a large gate. I loved it.

There was a maid to go with the house. Her name was Meilei; she was very sweet and spoke good English. The house had three bedrooms with traditional Japanese beds which rolled up, leaving the room full of space. Mr. Woo had no objections to our bringing in some of our own things and he made the written agreement with Father on the spot.

The area around the inside of the walls which enclosed the house was quite large. There were two lotus trees and many places to sit. The pond was actually fed by a stream that ran in under the back wall, then back out through the front.

Father said that we would move in on the next weekend. I begged to go up and tell Alistair that we had found a place. The driver took me while Father made a list of the things we would need to make this a comfortable home. Alistair was very glad that we could visit more often. He asked if Father had decided where I was going to school. At the moment, I wasn't enrolled yet at the embassy. I knew that there was a good Catholic school here in the village; that was where Alistair was going. I told him that I'd ask Father. On the drive back to the city, Father let it slip that he was going to enroll me in St. Andrews. I was so glad that I giggled. "You didn't think I'd make you rise at the crack of dawn to go into Tokyo for school, did you?" he asked in a merry tone of voice.

Father sent me out with one of the secretaries from the embassy to shop the next day for some of the things we would need. We bought a desk for Father and one for me; we found all the other essentials that Father had listed, except for a piano. We searched for a shop but didn't find one. When I told Father, he said he would find out where to look so we could go out the next day. It happened that when Father inquired, he discovered there were two pianos in the embassy that were not in use, so I was sent to try them out to see if one of them would do. The first was large and covered with roses carved in the front and down the legs It sounded like tin! The second was in the resident quarters of the guard house. It was light-colored wood. It, too, was carved, but with dragons whose eyes were jade. Even if it had sounded like tin I would have chosen it because of its sheer beauty.

The embassy had trucks available so the piano was taken out to the house. Now we needed a tuner. Back out into the steaming streets of the city the secretary and I went. Four music studios later, we found Mr. Chiang-sen, who first asked me to play for him. He led us down a hall at the side of the store and through a bright-colored silk hanging into a room that held the most beautiful piano I had ever laid eyes on. It was square, made of a red stained wood. It had dragons similar to the piano I had chosen, but these had glass eyes, and the legs of the piano were like dragon claws with great glass balls held in bright brass talons. I walked over and sat down. The keys were real ivory; the ebony keys shone with layers of shellac. I played a rondo. Mr. Chiang-sen said, "You like this piano? It makes you good music?" I admitted that it had a sound like I had never heard before; it sounded a bit like the Gulbransen that I played on at home, but more than that, it had a pitch that was near-perfect and a sound board that resonated like a grand piano. "I build inside myself!" Mr. Chiang-sen said, his hand gliding over the wood of the open top. "I come tune for you Saturday," he said, bowing deeply. "Maybe also you need teacher?" Without hesitation I said indeed I did. I explained that he could speak with my father when he came to tune the piano. We gave him the directions and he smiled. "I am living near this place. I ride bicycle everyday to come to studio." I was amazed; it was half an hour from the outskirts of the city by car, near an hour to the embassy because of the traffic in the streets. "Doesn't it take you a long time?" I queried. "No long, time for meditation," he said politely. I was not much acquainted with meditation but I thought to myself, it must be very difficult to meditate while weaving in and out of the horrendous traffic of the city, not to mention the noise and the animals and people on the roads.

I was satisfied that he would come and do a great job. I told Father over dinner about the piano and Mr. Chiang-sen. Father explained that lots of the people rode their bicycles everywhere. He said in fact he intended for both of us to get bikes right away, but that I would be restricted to riding mine from the house to school and around the village. I was never to go out on the highway toward Tokyo. That was fine with me. Tokyo was not a kind city; everyone rushed everywhere, the noise, the smells, and the crush of people were simply unpleasant.

We were glad when the weekend came. We set out Friday afternoon and arrived in the village long before dark. Mei-lei met us at the gate. She bowed politely and I bowed back. Our things had come along during the week and she had everything in place. The room that I had chosen now held a bamboo desk and seat as well as the traditional bed. There was a beautiful ink drawing of a lady under a bodi tree on one wall and near it, what I had thought to be a pipe. To my surprise, it now held long stems of lotus blossoms which reached up to nearly touch the low ceiling. It was very beautiful and so simple. I smiled. Mei-lei explained that it was a quiet place to sit and meditate. There was indeed a bench there with a lightly cushioned top. I was enthralled. I decided on the spot to learn about meditation.

Father's rooms too, were in order, and as I left my room I met him coming out into the garden at the corner of the pond. We walked around the house arm in arm, amazed that we had found such a great place. The sound of the water running over the little black stones and the gentle, quiet breeze all seemed to say "Welcome." We heard Mei-lei beckoning to us. We went into the dining room, which held a great red table and chairs, but she led us past it to a little room we hadn't noticed before. The room was lovely, with a tile floor and Japanese table and cushions that stood only a few inches off the floor. Mei-lei introduced us to a wonderful custom: the Tea Ceremony. We ate wonderful little rice cakes, some sushi, and drank the most delightful tea. There were blossoms floating in the bowls. As she served us, she explained what each part of the ceremony meant. At the end, I felt that I had rested, almost as if I had taken a nap. Little did I know that the ceremony was designed in such a way to induce a state of meditation.

When evening fell, the thin walls of the house shone with lights. What had appeared to be only white in the daylight now held secret water prints that gave the walls color and an inner light almost like a glass window. I fell asleep that night to the sound of the water running and the low chirping of night birds. I knew that this was going to be a magical place! It felt like my grandmother's house. That night, I dreamed of dragons, great winged ones, with eyes like those in the piano at Mr. Chiang-sen's shop. It seemed as if they were carrying me somewhere. I was awakened by the chatter of birds in the trees and the ringing of a gong somewhere outside.

Mr. Chiang-sen arrived bright and early. Father and Mei-lei were awake, but I was not. I hurriedly washed up and put on a nice, loose dress, combed my hair, and presented myself right in the middle of him loosening the pegs that held the front of the piano in place. He stopped what he was doing and bowed to me. "I make this inside also," he said, gesturing toward the inside, smiling. I left him there to go on with his work.

Father was sitting in the garden on a bench, sipping tea. Mei-lei immediately brought a cup for me, along with some almonds and some cut-up plums. "Very nice. You like, you see," she said as she set them down. Father said that he was impressed with Mr. Chiang-sen's promptness. I yawned, thinking that I would have liked a little more sleep. Maybe, to finish my dream. The time that Mr. Chiang-sen took to work on the piano was astonishing! When, after several hours, he called me in to play it, I was surprised. Now it had nearly the same quality of tone and resonance as the piano he had in the shop. "You like?" he asked, bowing slightly. "Yes, oh yes. Very much," I assured him. Father took him out to the garden to speak with him and to pay him for his labor. When he had gone, Father told me that he would be coming every Friday morning to give me lessons. I was glad; it would be nice to study with someone who knew about the insides of a piano.

The weekend was slow and quiet. I noted that Father looked more rested than he had in several weeks. This quick change had been difficult; he had very much wanted to go home for a time. As I grew older, I realized that even though Mother didn't seem to miss us, he missed her tremendously.

Monday morning, he took me to St. Andrews. The nuns who ran the school were Franciscans. They wore brown habits and walked with their heads down. But the principal, Sister Claire, was warm and pleasant. She accepted Father's account of my schooling along with the other needed paperwork and took me to be introduced to my first class. I had grown used to the sisters and the way they looked at the tiny Star of David that I wore around my neck. None of them ever tried to change my beliefs, but at times, they seemed to work around the issue as if testing what I knew about my own religion.

I was glad to get right into a school. It made the move seem easy for me. I loved studying, and when the sisters found out that I did, they really challenged me. It was the best part of being in a Catholic school, never being bored! Secretly, I was also pleased to be with Alistair. At lunch the first day, he took me outside the schoolyard to the garden the nuns had between the school and their convent. We ate on a bench under a blossoming cherry tree. I thought to myself that I was going to enjoy being here very much. Yes, very much indeed!

⇝ Chapter XIII

The village of Kirabashi was a clean, friendly place. There were more flowers of different types and blossoming trees than I had ever seen before. Life was gentler there in the countryside. One hardly could have guessed that there had been a terrible, ravaging war that tore through this country. I loved to ride about on my bike, often going into the village to shop in the outdoor stalls of the marketplace with Mei-lei. We would hunt for nice vegetables or stop at the fish lady's to pick out something for the evening meal. I had never eaten food like what she fixed; it felt clean and always tasted fresh. I tried my hand at the wok many times while we lived there but never could quite get the technique down. Father too remarked about the food, as it was always delicious. Mei-lei would smile politely when we complimented her but never say much.

One Saturday while we were in the village, we went to the dumpling man. It was the most wonderful stuff I had ever tasted; I could have eaten three of every one! Mei-lei explained to me that the rice flour used to make the dough was very light, unlike the flour we used at home, so these fairly melted in your mouth like angel puffs, quite unlike those I was used to at home. I wondered if I would be able to learn the delicate art of Japanese cooking. Everything was done so quietly, with such gentle movements of both hands and utensils. The days went by slowly there. I settled into a familiar routine: School from 8:00 A.M. to 4:00 P.M., time for studies, time for practice, and then time with Father if he arrived home before I went to bed. On Saturdays, I always had a lesson with Chiang-sen early in the morning. Usually, Father and I would bike up to visit with Alistair and his family, or they would come to visit with us. Alistair and I got on famously; we both loved our studies and both had outside interests as well. It was comfortable. The weather changed seasons in a different rotation than at home in the States. I woke one morning to torrential rain pounding on the roof, and the little stream nearly overflowed the pond.

I had never seen such rain; you could be perfectly dry one minute and the next be in a downpour. I learned to watch the clouds as they always formed at one end of the island and were easy to see moving towards us. I learned to carry my mackinaw in a pack on my bike, just in case.

Alistair and I went into Tokyo once in a while with our parents, but there was to be an exhibition in the Harbor of Tall Ships from the colonial days and we very much wanted to see it. Father agreed to take us and on the appointed time, the three of us headed for the city in the embassy car. There were more people than usual in the streets that day and as our car sat stalled in traffic, surrounded by the crush of vehicles, by humans on foot and on bikes, and by an array of various animals, we heard a loud explosion. It rocked the car and sent people scattering in all directions, shouting in their native tongue. Father couldn't see anything from inside the car so he ventured out to try and determine what the trouble was. He was back quickly, ordering our driver to turn around if possible and find a different route to the harbor. There was a long silence before Father began to tell us that the explosion had come from a fireworks factory, right beyond where we had been caught in the traffic, and that it appeared that people had been hurt. The knowledge that someone was suffering took some of the spirit from our excursion. Later we would learn that nearly forty people had been injured and nearly as many had died. Alistair wrote about it in our literature class the next week, as if he had been there and witnessed the whole thing. It bothered me that he would choose such a topic. Usually, his writing was free of any such harmful events.

He couldn't exactly explain but said he thought a lot lately about war and the like, so he just wanted to give it a try. The pieces were really good, but it still bothered me that he would use the event and turn it out so roughly, as if he had seen such things. We discussed it a lot in the days that followed. I had written about the Tall Ships without so much as a mention of the event. Eventually I shared it with Father and he tried to help me thorough the whys, stating matter-of-factly that, "If Alistair goes home to go to university, he may well end up in the service, so it's not unusual for a lad of his age to write about violence."

I accepted Father's explanation and put it out of my mind. I loved life in the little village of Kirabashi; people were pleasant and kind to each other. There were many people whom I came to know there, but perhaps the most important person was an old woman named Tang Lee. She was not Japanese but Chinese and had come as a stowaway when she was a teen. Later she married a Japanese man and together they raised four children. She now had eighteen grandchildren and still worked in the fish market that her husband ran. We would visit over bowls of rice and steamed fish, trading stories about life and where it might take us next. She said she never felt completely at home anywhere until they had moved to this little village when she was just twenty. It was long ago and the village had changed over the years, she told me. But "the heart of her never changed!" she stated emphatically. "A place lives just like we do. It breathes, this earth we stand on," she'd tell me smilingly and gently tap the ground with her tiny feet.

I found her one day, sitting under a great bodi tree on a bench. At first I thought she was sleeping. She was, however, meditating, so I asked her if she would teach me how, and she did. "Meditation just breathing, you watch Tang. In and out, slow and deliberate. You watch your own breath and suddenly you are far away from here." I tried it. Sure enough, when you watch your breath and breathe deliberately, soon you find that you are sort of floating in the air, as Tang said . . . far away . . . I liked the sensation very much. I tried to share the idea with Alistair but he laughed and said, "You may meditate, I'll take a bike ride!" So I learned, and he never tried it. It was okay, I guess. Young men have different ideas about how to relax.

Tang taught me other things too: how to follow my breath with my body, doing all sorts of posture and positions. It's called Tai Chi. It does wonderful things for your being: It slows down your thinking and relaxes your whole self, body, soul, mind and spirit. I practiced daily at home, at school, and with Tang.

Father laughed too, seeing me one morning in the garden stretching like a great cat on the wall. He laughed so hard he tumbled over. But I kept up with the practice and felt my body growing with each stretch, each hour of meditation until I could see results in the mirror: a body as limber as a willow twig, lithe like a ballet dancer, and a mind always open to new ideas, new ways of seeing life.

Alistair finished his high school diploma. He wrote off for University applications and after a few weeks declared that he would enter Harvard in the fall. I felt sad, but when I shared my feelings with Tang she said, "All birds fly. If he is supposed to, he will fly back here. If he doesn't, you will flex your wings and go on." The logic of that stayed with me and salved my heart when, at the end of the summer in August, he left for the States. I didn't know then that I would never see him again. I think if I had, I would have told him that I loved him.

At first there were letters almost every day, then only a letter a week, until finally there were no more letters. I continued to flourish in school. Mr. Chiang-sen wanted me to learn another instrument so I began to try to conquer the violin.

The results devastated the peace and quiet of our house and anyone within earshot! After several weeks, I gave up. Then Mr.

Chiang-sen tried to teach me the flute. He thought it was "Very important, Miss, have more than one instrument!" The flute at least became pleasant in a short while so that those around me didn't suffer!

Tang went on teaching me how to be a lady. She would comb my curly hair into marvelous shapes and even taught me how to make up my face. One day she took me to the kimono maker who was her friend. They put me in a traditional dress with an obi tied round. I couldn't believe how elegant I looked. Next evening, I asked Father if I could have the money to buy a kimono. He gave that and more, saying simply, "You never ask me for much and seem to find your pleasure in people more than in things." He took me into Tokyo the next day and I got my own bank account. I was thrilled.

When next I visited Tang, we made plans to spend a day with the kimono maker. I knew just what I had in mind: a soft, pink kimono with white lotus flowers, a brighter-colored obi, and silk flowers to match for my hair. I wanted to have a picture with Tang. It was odd but since Alistair left, she was truly my best friend. Amazing how two people separated by fifty years can become so caught up in each other's lives. Maybe it was my need for a mother or her need for the daughter she never had, having had all boys. It certainly made for an easy fit. We both enjoyed life in the village, and it was certainly nice to have an older woman to whom I could turn when I needed the kind nurturing of a mother figure.

One afternoon, I arrived home from school to find Mei-lei waiting for me in the garden. "The kimono lady wants to see you right away!" she told me. I hurried to change from my school uniform and rode my bike into the village. I rode past the fish market to see if Tang could accompany me, but to my surprise the market was closed. I rode on to the kimono makers. Madame Lee looked up from her machine as I entered. Taking off the little glasses she used to follow her stitching, she rose and came to me. "Little one, we have great tragedy," she spoke softly. "Tang husband, he die this morning. Tang is very much upset. I want to take you to her." I had never been to Tang's home; I had no idea where she lived. We always met under the bodi tree or at the market, but I had no fear of going with Madame Lee. As we rode through the streets, Madame Lee explained that because Tang had no daughters, there would be no place for her in the funeral ceremonies. The custom seemed strange but I listened intently as Madame Lee spoke, as I wanted to know as much information as she was willing to share so that I would be able to do the correct things for my friend. She explained that the men would carry out the needed traditions but that Tang needed us to help her with her mourning.

When we arrived at the house, I was amazed to see that it was a home of wealth. There were several gardens and many outdoor seating arrangements. I didn't notice anyone about until we turned the corner to enter a tiny gate in a wall. There sat my friend on a mat on the ground, under the shadow of a Buddha that sat on a niche in the trunk of a lotus tree. She was dressed in white with a dark sash and was on her knees, bent forward until her forehead rested on the ground. I decided to watch Madame Lee and follow her lead. She walked to the edge of the mat, removed her sandals, and knelt down on one side of Tang, who remained motionless until I had positioned myself on the other side of her. She rose from her waist to a kneeling position. I could see great tears had already fallen on the mat and marked her china face. She began to chant in Chinese a song that sounded as if her heart was broken. It went on for a long while. Finally, she stopped and returned to her previous position. Madame Lee now took up the same pose; I followed suit. After what seemed hours, Tang rose and offered each of us a hand as we struggled up from the strained position.

She was quiet, no longer crying. I offered her my arms and she let herself lean against me. I hugged her tight, not knowing what to say. There seemed no words in English that were appropriate and the words I knew in Yiddish escaped my mind in this moment of need. She turned to Madame Lee and spoke softly,

"Thank you. I very glad you bring my Leah; she is like daughter to me."

We went inside the house and I realized that it would soon be dark. Father would not know where I was and would be terribly worried. I told Madame Lee and she found a boy who worked for Mr. Tang who spoke good English. I wrote a note to Father, explaining, and he sped off on his bike to deliver it. We sat in silence with Tang, sipping tea. There were lots of people around but none of them came near to where we sat. I thought that some of the faces in the group looked familiar and realized that they must be sons, wives, and grandchildren.

From another room toddled in a small girl, maybe four or five years old. She first went to one of the ladies and then came over to us. She spoke to Tang in Japanese then crawled into her lap and began to suck her thumb. My father arrived in the car shortly and was brought in by the same boy we had sent with the message. Father greeted the young men in the group, Tang's sons, before he came over to us.

He asked if there was anything he could do. Tang thanked him and said that I had come to help her cry, and that was enough. I hugged Tang again and she asked Father if it would be alright if I could attend the funeral the next morning. Father hesitated but decided that it would be fine. Madame Lee was leaving too, so Father had our bicycles put in the trunk and we drove Madame Lee home.

We rode in silence most of the way back to the house. Father said that after dinner, he would explain the ceremony that I would witness tomorrow so that I would know what was going to happen. He said that he would like me to stay with Madame Lee and to wait afterward at the house until he came for me. I agreed.

Climbing into my bed that night, I thought about all the things I had learned in my life up till now. I recalled the funeral of the boy at the dells and wondered about death. I woke in the night several times, thinking of my friend Tang. I wondered how she must feel, having lived forty-six years of her life with this man and now finding herself alone.

The lessons of courage and strength that I would learn the next day would carry me through many such losses of my own. I would come to understand that death is not the end of self; it is only another change along the path that our spirit and soul take on their way back to their Creator.

Chapter XIV

I woke early and found that Madame Lee had sent round a kimono. It was cream-colored with a pale gray obi. Mei-lei helped me fix my unruly curls into a nice roll and helped me dress. Father had sent the car and driver back to take me to Madame Lee's. I was sad but not nervous. Father had explained the details of the Buddhist service for cremation and I felt that I was ready for whatever lay ahead. Madame Lee and I rode to Tang's in heavy silence. We arrived just as the four sons did, and the eldest held the car door for us and thanked us for coming to his mother's aide. We all walked in to find Tang waiting, eyes swollen with crying. She came to us and we both hugged her tightly. The oldest son came to take us to the bier. It would be Tang's only time with her deceased husband. The body lay on a bed of flowers, his eyes closed, hands clasped across his chest. He was in a white kimono and against the background of bright red and white gladioli, he looked like royalty. Madame Lee and I knelt on bamboo mats at the entrance to the room. Tang walked up to coffin; she laid her head against his hands and whispered to him in Chinese. She didn't cry; she stood there a long while, resting her head against him until finally she kissed him on the forehead and turned toward us. Her eyes shone like bright diamonds, tears sitting just on the edge of tumbling over. She said nothing. We rose and went to her. She took a hand from each of us and we walked out to the waiting family and friends.

The sons carried the coffin from the house to the Buddhist temple in the middle of the village. There were several monks outside waiting for our arrival. The coffin, which seemed to be a shallow box, was placed in position and the ceremony began.

There was much chanting, and some speeches which I could not understand because I did not know the language. There was a wooden tablet on a pallet beside the body, and all the flowers were white and red. One large bouquet of red and white gladioli sat against the coffin. Across them was a white ribbon; printed on it in red letters was the name of Tang's husband in Japanese. I recognized it from the sign over his shop. The service was long but finally, the top of the coffin was brought out and nailed in place. The coffin was now carried by some older men from the village, preceded by a monk carrying a white banner. We followed behind the procession of family out to the cemetery, where the coffin was placed on a pyre made of red bricks. There were more chants and prayers, and then all of the family who had brought candles made into bunches went forward and stood by the pyre. Tang held tight to my hand, taking me along as she went up to the very end of the pyre. She held a group of candles which resembled a torch, and in among them she had woven bits of laurel twigs and cinnamon bark. She whispered something in Chinese and then stooped and tossed the burning bundle under the pyre. Her sons and their families did the same. In only a few seconds, the fire was reaching up around the coffin on all sides. I watched intently. There was a sweet smell in the air mingled with the scent of incense and fragrant wood. In a short time there would be nothing left but ashes which I learned later from Madame Lee would be gathered up by the sons and some of it buried in the cemetery under a little shrine, while the rest would be buried in other places.

Our return to the house was solemn but not as quiet as when

we walked to the temple. Inside, the house had been transformed in our absence; it now resembled a place where a great festival might take place. As we entered, we were showered with salt. I learned that it was a sort of purification meant to ward off any other evil event or bad thing that might befall the family. There was an altar set up with a picture of Tang's husband when he had been much younger as a soldier; there were flowers and incense burning on the small, lacquered table.

Now the atmosphere turned into one of celebration. There was much to eat and drink, and the oldest son seemed to be the center of attention. I stayed near Tang while Madame Lee went to and fro, bringing us delicacies to taste and sweet cups of tea which smelled of Jasmine, with blossoms floating in them. There was much noise and when I remarked about it, Tang explained that this was customary so that nothing else would befall them. It was their belief that the noise would drive away bad luck or evil entities. It was after dark when Father arrived for me but much later when we actually left, as the sons of Tang wanted him to eat and talk with them about America. Tang, Madame Lee, and I had retired to one of the small side rooms, away from the bustle, and were all resting when Father came to say it was time to leave.

Tang gave me a little booklet with Buddhist things in it. She bowed deeply to my father in an expression of thankfulness. My Father bowed back then reached into his pocket to pull out a red envelope which he handed Tang. She bowed again and we were escorted to the car by all the sons. We gave Madame Lee a ride back to her home. She told Father that he should be proud to have such a strong and virtuous daughter. I wondered what she meant, but I was nearly asleep and didn't ask.

That night I dreamed of dragons again, and of home and my grandmother. I wondered what she would have thought of my attendance at the funeral. I asked Father next morning about the envelope that he had given Tang. He explained that in most of the countries of the Far East, it is a custom to give some cash to help with the expense of the funeral, the wake, and the use of the temple and priests. He told me that he wanted to do this not only because of the appropriateness, but because he could tell that I loved Tang very much. At school the next day, I realized that three of the teenage boys who had been at Tang's house were in my class. When we had our morning break, one of them came over to where I was sitting. "Hello," he said quietly. "You were at my grandfather's funeral. I wanted to thank you. I see you often when you study with my grandmother, but now I feel like you are a part of my family." Chen-lei sat down beside me and we began to talk about the funeral. He explained things that I hadn't understood, like the lighting of the bier. Later that day, we went to visit his grandmother in the shop; she was so glad to see us come in. She smiled. "Now you have new friend, I think!" she said to Chen-lei. I watched as he put on an apron and started to help his grandmother cut up some fish. He is handsome, I thought to myself. Quiet in school, he studies hard like Alistair and never jokes or gets into any kind of trouble. I wondered why I hadn't noticed him before.

Our friendship flourished. Chen-lei and I had much more in common than just his grandmother: He played the piano, the flute and the lyre, a sort of small lap harp that made wonderful sounds. He loved poetry and life in the country and was just brilliant when it came to history. He thought that the entire world should have had to study the effects of the Second World War so that we shouldn't ever have another such grave disaster. He said in private that he did not approve of the way his father acted at his grandfather's funeral. He felt that women were equally as capable and smart and should never be made to feel inferior.

I very much enjoyed my newfound friendship, so much so that I asked Father if it would be all right with him to ask Chen-lei to dinner. Father thought it a grand idea and suggested that we invite Madame Lee and Tang also. I set about making plans, careful to count the forty-one days of mourning so that Tang would be able to come. Little did I suspect that I would meet another form of prejudice here in this country, which seemed so civil and so pleasant!

⇝ Chapter XV

Life went slowly back to its normal routine. I tried to visit Tang everyday in the afternoon. She seemed to go along all right. She worked at the market just as she had done with her husband, but now the eldest son also worked there several days a week also. He was Chen-lei's father. He clearly did not approve of the friendship that was growing between his son and me. He would turn away when he saw me enter the shop. Tang would scold him in her cryptic Japanese, and then mutter to herself in her native Chinese.

Chen-lei and I often meditated with Tang in the afternoon under the bodi tree. She really enjoyed the two of us and often told us stories from her past, or of her husband and her when they were young. My kimono was nearly finished and Madame Lee sent for me for the final touches of length of sleeve and hem. I spent a fun afternoon with her. She laughed when I wondered how the women sat down. "This is why you see us sit on knees," she explained. "Is easier with obi than sit on chair." The kimono was beautiful; it was a silk of the lightest shade of pink, and through the cloth there were pink and white lotus blossoms and tiny twigs with light-green leaves. The obi was a much darker pink of the same shade and was bound to a piece of green cloth the exact color of the leaves. It was an altogether beautiful sight. I needed a pair of Japanese sandals. Tang went with me to get them. I picked plain ones with a stiff sole; they were very comfortable. I could hardly wait to show Father. When at last it was finished, I carried it home on my bike. I asked Mei-lei to fix a tea ceremony. When Father came home, she ushered him into the little room and I helped her serve the tea. He was impressed. "This kind of education doesn't come from a textbook," he said, smiling over his rice cakes. I talked with him about everything so of course I shared the way that Chen's father reacted every time he saw me. Father tried his best diplomatic explanations, but in the end he had to admit that it was because I was white, but even more because I was an American.

Father agreed to let me have a picture with Tang. He said that he would find a photographer and that he would arrange for there to be two copies of the best photo, so that I could give one to her. I was ahead of my class at school, and so the principal gave me a special assignment: to write about everything that I had learned from the people I met living in the village. I wrote about Tang, the funeral, Chen-lei and his father, about the kimono and Madame Lee. Sister Clair was very impressed,; she said it was the best paper she'd ever read. She was concerned that I understand the wall between the Japanese and America, so she had me read about the Japanese and their role in the Second World War, about the bombing of Hiroshima and Nagasaki. I began to understand. One day, when I went into the fish market, Tang was not there. For the first time, her son had to speak to me. I took the advantage and told him a little about myself. He listened politely. "I know you very good girl, excel in studies of all sorts. You I not dislike, I dislike that my son like you so very much. I once love American girl. She was a reporter. My father was very outspoken with me; he made me leave off my friendship and not see her any more." There was a long silence between us. Finally, he said, "Friendship is okay, no problem with friendship! I try not to be rude to you. I am thankful very much to you for your friendship with my mother, and maybe I think with my son too. Chen very smart but not have many friends. We start new, you and I, okay?" he asked, looking right into my eyes. I said, "Of course, okay". He gave me a gorgeous, fresh white fish and told me to ask Mei-lei to make it for my father.

Father was pleased. He said that I had been brave to speak out. Most women in Japan never say anything to a man. Father was pleased too that Quan had sent along the fish. He explained that it was like a peace offering in case Father had been upset with his treatment of me. Early the next morning, I went to meet Chen-lei. We were going to see the Koi at a special pool inside one of the Buddhist temples. When I arrived at the back of the fish shop, Quan was waiting with Chen-lei. He asked if I would mind if he went with us; he had a plan for a special surprise. I loved any sort of surprise and so I thought it grand that he would take time from the shop to go with us.

We all three rode our bikes. The ride was about six kilometers. The temple was very old and sat on a hill looking down on the village, and from the place where we were, you could see a long way in all directions. We toured the pools of Koi; they were the most beautiful fish I had ever seen. Chen's father showed us how the Koi loved to be handled. Rolling back his sleeves, he put his hand into the water and a great, black, red-and-white fish swam right into them, letting him lift her to the edge of the water so that we could stroke her sides. I was amazed. When we finished touring the pools, it was nearly noon. I had brought some fruit and rice but Quan said no, he was taking us to a special lunch. We were walking out of the gardens toward our bikes when he turned us toward the great monastery doors. We left our shoes on the steps and slipped inside. There in the main room was the most beautiful Gold Buddha that I had ever seen. He must have been at least twelve feet high. He was surrounded by small altars bearing all sorts of offerings; incense burned there and candles too. We walked through the temple and, to my surprise, out into a garden, where one of the monks who had led some of the service for Tang's husband sat on a bench.

He rose and came toward us. Quan greeted him in Japanese and then turned to introduce me. The monk was Chen-lei's youngest uncle. I was very humbled to be greeted with a bow from a monk. He led us to a small house in the center of the garden, where we were served in the tradition of the tea ceremony by a young woman who had a shaved head and wore a yellow robe. It was all very lovely. Quan spoke with his brother and then translated for me. His brother had lived here in the monastery for over ten years now. I admired his courage and his obedience. Chen explained that his uncle spent most of his time praying and working in the gardens.

The day was over much too soon. I felt that I had been very privileged and thanked Quan for the honor he had shown me. He said that he thought I was deserving of such a day, and that it had pleased him to see that I knew so many of the customs of his country. That night over dinner, I rambled on about my day until it suddenly struck me that Father was very quiet and solemn. "Is there anything wrong?" I asked him. Father leaned his elbows on the table, placed his two hands together as he always did when he was thinking or pondering a problem. After a few moments, he began. "We'll be leaving here in a month's time," he started slowly. "I don't think that this will be easy for you. You have really grown to love this village and the people here; you have made friends and most of all, you have grown much.

Your schooling has gone well. I've already spoken with Sister Clair; she says that you could go into your senior year of high school at home in the States and still be the head of your class. In fact she said that you would be more than ready and might be bored. I don't know what is going to come up next. Our government at home is involved in this mess in Vietnam. I'm not sure where I might be sent next. We have to discuss what you want to do. I don't expect you to make a decision right now, but I want you to start to think about whether you want to live at home in San Francisco with your mother for your senior year, or maybe spend it in a boarding school. I don't want to influence your decision . . . you are old enough to make it yourself."

When Father stopped talking, I was speechless. I guess I had stopped thinking about the States, about returning home. Maybe I had let my mind think that I might stay here in this lovely, simple place forever. I didn't know what I wanted except that at that moment, I needed to speak with Tang or Tante Rivka or . . . I didn't realize it but I was crying. Father put his big hand over my small ones lying on the table, folded. "I know this will be hard for you. Take a few days; we have time. If you need to discuss things, let me know."

With that, he handed me his handkerchief and I broke into great sobs. This was the first time in my life that I had really become attached. This place and all its graciousness, its beauty, and its kindness had taken root inside of me. Father didn't say anything more and when I finally gained control of myself, I simply asked to be excused from the table. I went out into the garden and found the meditation bench near the back, which had a little pagoda with Buddha sitting on it. I unrolled the mat that hung there and knelt down. Without thinking, I bent all the way forward and let my forehead rest on the mat. It was a singular act of growth and grief. I knew that I didn't pray to Buddha but I felt that my G-d, the G-d of Abraham, Isaac and Jacob would welcome this position of supplication.

How long I knelt there I do not know, but when I rose from my position to my knees, Tang and Madame Lee were kneeling close by. I realized that they were there because my father had sent for them. I guess he no longer knew how to deal with a nearly grown daughter and thought that the job was best left to the two women who had become like mothers to me. They rose and came to me, each lending me a hand. We went inside to my rooms and Tang brought a bowl of sweet, scented water and washed my face, Madame Lee excused herself to go to the kitchen to bring tea.

I learned that day the value of true friendship. When you have a need and help appears, there is such a comfort in its presence. We talked almost until the light of dawn had crept across the sky; we took a walk into the village to the temple and heard the first chants of a new day; we cooled our feet in the stream that ran through the temple garden; we shared thoughts about how it would feel to move on. Tang told me that I must be brave, that courage only grows in us from trials. Madame Lee spoke to me about how life is a golden bowl and that it holds all of our experiences. They never leave us; how we are able to draw strength from what we know. I talked about my mother, about how she couldn't love me, about Tante Rivka and how I knew she was my real mother without anyone telling me. We talked and talked. At last I was exhausted. Tang walked me back to my house and tucked me into my bed. When I awoke, it was afternoon. Tang was sitting on the floor, head on her knees, asleep. She awoke and came over to where I was standing. "We have no more time for tears now; we must begin to get you ready," she said, looking over my shoulder at me in the mirror.

Father, true to his word, arranged for a photographer, and Tang and I had a picture taken. The photographer made two copies in 8x10 size. Father bought me a set of lovely bamboo frames. On the second Wednesday of that month, we had no school so I planned to take Tang's picture over and spend the day in the shop. She was so thrilled with the gift, her eyes nearly brimmed over, once again giving them the same appearance they had on the day her husband was cremated.

We worked all morning in the shop. I didn't see Chen-lei or his father and I wondered where they were. A little past noon, Tang said that we were going to close the shop and go to her home for a little rest and something to eat. We locked my bike in the cutting room and walked the distance in the bright sunshine.

I noticed that there were several bikes at the side of the entrance to Tang's home but I thought nothing about it. Even when we walked into the entrance garden, I noticed nothing unusual, but when we entered the main room of the house, I could not believe my eyes! There were flowers and bright candles everywhere. The room was full of all my classmates, the nuns from the school, Chen and his father, Madame Lee ... everyone who I knew and loved from the village was there. Tang and Quan along with the nuns and Madame Lee had made this plan. It was like a festival. Everyone had brought flowers or other small tokens for me to say farewell and to let me know they would miss me. Chiang-sen played music as did some of the others. We had such a great time; the party went on and on. Others came. Father arrived from town. He had known about the plan too. I received many gifts. Chen-lei gave me a beautiful pair of pearl earrings; each held two great pearls, one dark gray; the other white. His father and grandmother gave me a necklace to match. It held exactly thirty six gray and white pearls and the clasp was a beautiful gold dragon with diamonds set in his eyes. Later I would learn that it had been Tang's; her husband had given it to her on their thirty-sixth anniversary. Each gift in some way represented the giver; each had an individual meaning, and I was overwhelmed with the generosity of each one.

My father, in true diplomatic style, had arranged for an appropriate gift for me to give each in return: a little book about America, with a red leather cover, and in the inside cover he had printed my home address and an open invitation to visit us. Food arrived from all over the village. Mei-lei and others had arranged to provide dinner for the now very large crowd. I felt very humble. Chen's uncle, the monk, gave me a special blessing. Then I was supposed to speak to everyone, Tang said, so I tried to tell them how much I loved the village and its people. I told them that someday, I would return there.

Finally, people started to leave. Madame Lee told me that it was customary for me to say goodbye to everyone one at a time. By the time the last folks left, it was midnight. Father and Tang's sons loaded the gifts into the car while I tried to thank Tang and Madame Lee. On the ride home, my heart was so full. Years later, I would hear someone say that it takes a village to raise a child, and I would remember this day.

⇒ Chapter XVI

The next two weeks were very hectic. We packed our things for shipping, held back the things we needed to carry with us and before I could think about it, we were standing in the garden saying goodbye to our friends. Tang, Madame Lee, Quan and Chen-lei, Mr. Chieng-sen; they all came. There were hugs all around and then the deep bowing done as was the custom. My eyes burned with tears and my heart ached inside me. We drove quietly out of the village, down the road to Tokyo. The silence was good; it helped me to quiet myself as Tang had taught me, but I wasn't able to stop my mind from thinking that I might never see any of them again! Father had arranged for a stop in Israel, and again this was a very good thing. Tante Rivka met us at the airport. She looked older somehow; her hair at the edges now was turning silver. I was grateful for her warm hug and sweet greeting.

We stayed in Israel for two weeks. I spent every moment I could with Tante Rivka, and Father went to visit friends at the embassy and often was gone all day. I tried to tell her how it felt to leave my friends, and she tried to help me see that life is a chain of events, ever evolving with or without our help. We talked about what I should do, whether I should stay with Mother or go to a boarding school. She didn't like the idea that I should be in boarding school and expressed concern that I had never had the experience of a regular school. I very much wanted to go somewhere away from San Francisco though, and she understood.

We went to the temple and celebrated Shabbat. It felt good but somehow foreign to me. Afterward, as we walked back to her house, I related the experience of the night that Father told me we would be leaving Kirabashi. She said that she had felt that urge to prostrate herself many times and that often she did so in the privacy of her own rooms.

Tante Rivka spent a lot of time teaching me about the Holocaust this trip. She said I was old enough to understand what had happened, old enough to begin to communicate with Mother about it when I got home. She told me all the awful horrible parts that until now I had only guessed at; she explained to me that there were lots of people who went crazy from the sheer horror of it all. I asked about her life before the war. She told me that she was a Rabbi's wife and that she had three children: a baby girl that she knew died and two sons who she felt were probably killed or died.

A lot of the things she shared with me during that stay made me feel closer to her than ever. I still had my one question, but it simply wasn't the time to ask, or maybe I wasn't ready yet to know.

I loved being in Jerusalem with her. We saw things in the same way, it seemed. One evening, we went walking and we happened to pass a group of nuns. Not thinking, I said "Hello, Sisters." She looked at me and slowly began to laugh. "My little mixed-up lady," she giggled. "I wonder that you even know who you are; your education has taken such a different road than most." I had to laugh too. I had attended mostly Catholics schools, had been exposed to Hindu beliefs in South Africa, Buddhists beliefs in Japan, and yet I thought myself to be a good Jew. I giggled at the exposé that ran through my mind; she threw back her head and laughed with me. It was wonderful!

I really hated to leave but finally the day came. Father and I boarded the plane for New York; we would go to Washington D.C. first and on to California at the end of the next week. I felt lonely, I felt cold, and besides that, I felt frightened . . . it had been a long while since I had seen Mother. I had changed a lot, grown not just in body but in the heart and soul of me. I wondered what she would think and if she would notice how very much I had changed.

When we went through customs in New York, Father declared all the items that we had brought with us that were of value, but he forgot that I was wearing my earrings. They hadn't been out of my ears since I got them. The officer kept looking at me and asking Father if he was sure that was all. Finally he pointed to my ear. "And these?" he questioned sternly. "Don't these match the necklace?" Father said that he forgot I was wearing them. The officer looked at him sternly and called for his supervisor; he whispered something to him and then motioned toward us. We were ushered into a little room while every pocket of every bag was turned inside out. Finally, they came to Father's coat pocket. When they opened his ID wallet, their faces turned bright red! "Excuse our ignorance, Mr. McRyan," the supervisor lamely apologized. Father just looked at him, not saying a word. Then he took his little notepad out and wrote down the officer's name. We were helped out to the car. Father laughed as we drove off. "I won't file a complaint," he said, "but I wanted to make them think about it when they are rude to the next person!" Father was like that. It was a part of him that I didn't quite understand, and sometimes I didn't care for it.

We spent time with my aunt and uncle in New York. They remarked about how terribly "grown up" I looked. We went to see a play off Broadway that dealt with the racial issues in America. I said afterward that I thought it was very unintelligent for people to think badly about others because of the color of their skin. Uncle Brad scolded me. He said that I should never make such remarks, especially not in public.

Father tried to tell me how things were at home, but I simply refused to believe that people could be ignorant enough to think themselves better simply because they were white! Would I be in for some surprising times ahead?

I muddled through the week in D.C. It was hot, humid, and the crowds of summer were everywhere. I hated most of it and thought that I would like to run straight back to Kirabashi.

Life here was a rush; there was never any time to reflect. People didn't speak when you spoke unless they knew you. People honked and yelled obscenities when traffic got slow. I saw a man punch another in the face on Washington Square one afternoon. What was wrong with them? I wondered. Finally we boarded a plane for California. I was anxious. I had been very careful getting ready; I had gone shopping in New York and bought a black-and-white plaid suit that had a silk blouse in light yellow. The salesgirl who helped me said it was the latest fashion. I wore little patent leather opera pumps, dark stockings, and finished it with a prim little purse that matched the shoes.

When we were going down the ramp into the airport waiting room, I spotted Mother in the crowd, and near by was Ann. Mother was dressed to the T's in a very elegant navy blue dress, white and navy shoes, and a little pillbox-type hat sat perched on her head. Gosh! I thought to myself. She hasn't seen us; I bet I could walk right by and she wouldn't know it was me.

As it turned out, Ann spotted us before Mother and reached us before Mother did, so that I was fully engulfed in Ann's great hug when Mother came up to us. She greeted my father with a kiss; he smiled from ear to ear. She looked at me and said, "My dear, you should never wear colored blouses with black and white, it just isn't done!"

No hug, no hello, no it's good to see you . . . same Mother I had left nearly three years ago. But unlike the girl who had begged to go off with her father and would have said nothing, I bristled and then I said, "Hello, Mother, it's nice to see you too. Did you miss us?" She gave me "the look," and Father rested his hand on my arm, as if to say "don't start."

The house looked wonderful; my room was just as I had left it except for a new rug. Ugh! I sighed. Pink roses on a navy blue background! I set about putting away some of my things and decided that I would speak to Father about maybe going to see Grandmother right away . . . I just didn't want to be here.

I unrolled a pair of slacks that I had packed around the picture of Tang and I suddenly realized that I now knew what it meant to be homesick. If it had been possible, I would have taken the first plane I could find back to Tokyo.

Dinner that first night was a large meal of prime rib roast with all the trimmings. I didn't feel like eating but I managed to struggle through. I realized afterward that it was a mistake. On the trip home, I had chosen what to eat and where, usually sticking to the clean food of the Japanese or having a salad. I got sick, I had never been so sick to my stomach. I was sick for several days. The food was too rich, the Doctor said. I simply wasn't used to all the animal fat. "My goodness, Elizabeth!" Mother frowned. "You've turned into one of those Orientals you became so fond of!" I merely groaned with pain and took to my bed.

Ann took care of me while I recovered. Mother came to my room only once in three days, that was to tell me that I was going to miss a 'splendid' dinner at the Club. I felt glad to be sick!

Since we came home at the end of July, there was plenty of time for me to go to Grandmother's for a while. And go I did! Father bought me a plane ticket to Madison, Mother said goodbye from the steps of the house, and I was Free again! I had dressed casual for the plane ride: a pair of cargo pants ala Indiana Jones, a simple red gabardine shirt, my hair up in a bun, and a pair of laced oxfords. I had suffered through Mother giving me the look and was ever grateful to Ann who said she thought I looked quite "smart."

When I arrived in Madison, my Uncle Lloyd and Grandmother met me at the airport! Unlike my mother who obviously couldn't remember what I looked like and didn't care, Grandmother was waving both hands in the air the minute I stepped out of the plane's door onto the ramp. I hurried through the crowd right into her great pine-scented arms! She held me tight for a long time, then stepped back and said, "I do believe my real girl is here!" I recalled now what it felt like to be home!

We chattered away gaily all the way out to the dells. We stopped at the market to pick up something, and I saw a face that looked only vaguely familiar. "Charlie?" I asked, hesitating. "Charlie, is that really you?" He turned and looked at me. Recognition crept slowly across his handsome face. "Well, aren't you the sight, though?'" he responded, grabbing me and giving me a great hug! Everyone around us stared. "Are you here for the rest of the summer?" he asked politely, disentangling himself from me. "Yes, and maybe more," I said, moving on to catch up with Grandmother. Charlie picked up his two bags and called over his shoulder. "Wait till I tell Ella, and Pa!"

Ah, the sense of being at home, of coming back to that place that you have known for years, of being recognized and loved unconditionally. I felt the warmth of the moment with my entire being. Grandmother was glad we had seen Charlie; she said there was going to be a powwow this coming weekend and we would go.

We gathered our groceries and left the market, piled back into Uncle Lloyd's car, and headed for home. I was so excited. Grandmother had sent me some pictures of the door, but in a few moments I could see for myself. I asked Uncle Lloyd if he could stop just short of the bend in the road and let me out so that I could walk; he did. I hadn't gone four steps when Blackie and Spot came tramping out of the trees, tails wagging. They greeted me as if I had only been away to town on an errand. I took my time. I even slowed down; I wanted to be able to savor the quiet, the sound of the sighing of the wind in the pines reminded me of the garden in Kirabashi. The smell was fresh and sweet. Here and there, a bird twittered or a chipmunk called his warning. "Man in the wood," he sang out, alerting everyone! I turned the corner in the road and there stood the house . . . sun shining on it in the late afternoon, and just as I remembered – the window shone like a kaleidoscope, the colors reflecting onto the steps and the porch! I stood perfectly still, letting the magic of the place soothe me. I walked slowly on after a few minutes. The lake sparkled as the late afternoon breeze blew across its surface. I thought of all the wonderful good times I had had here. Of my cousins, my friends at the reservation, and of Grandmother. I wondered what I would have been like now if it hadn't been for her and my father.

Grandmother came out on to the porch. She watched as I made slow, deliberate progress up the path toward the house. She stood there and once more, I wondered how she stayed so timeless in a world that is always pushing us forward.

When I reached the steps, Grandmother held out her arms. I went to her and she began to waltz across the porch, just as she had on the day I first found myself being twirled round on the dance floor at my parents' wedding. Magic! I thought to myself. Being home is magic. It's as though they never change: the people here, the place itself. While I have been out in this great world of ours learning new customs, seeing new things, everything here just waits for me to return.

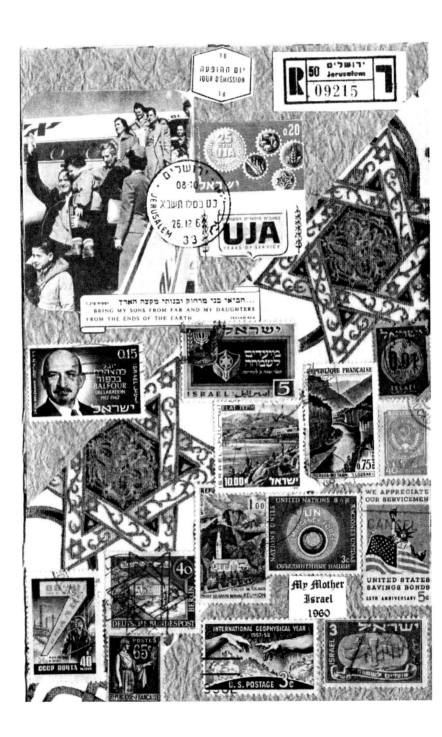

⊱ Chapter XVII

It was easy being back at the lake; things were as they had always been. Up at dawn most mornings, we ate a good breakfast and did the chores. The only thing missing was the old gray goose. The first morning there, I went out to the hen house to feed the chickens and gather eggs. I noticed right away that he was absent. Not that I had liked being picked on, but he was a part of the life I knew and I actually had looked forward to having him run after me. Grandmother said that one day, he wandered out of the hen yard and never came back. She suspected that a wolf or maybe a fox had killed him. Surprising how something like that makes you feel sad. It just wasn't the same going out to get eggs. I guess over the years, we had formed a bond, that old goose and I.

Grandmother had a large garden every summer. This year's was no exception. There were over thirty different kinds of vegetables growing there. We'd weed a bit, pick the things that were ripe, water and prune the bugs from the large leafed plants . . . it was all very simple and calming. I thought to myself that in many ways, it was a form of meditation, walking in and out of the rows in silence, tending the plants as they needed it.

Everyone knew I was home. We got invitations to dinner from a dozen places or so. For the most part, we turned them down except for the powwow. We went up to the reservation with a great load of vegetables and eggs. We stayed for the weekend. I had so much fun; we danced and ate, rode horseback out into the valley up the river, nearly twenty miles. Charlie and I went fly-fishing with a bunch of his friends, and I smoked my first cigarette. Mother would be furious if she knew. I had often sat with my grandmother on the back steps after dinner when she would light her pipe with a sweet-smelling tobacco. I would savor the smell as it drifted on the cool, fresh breezes. I didn't enjoy the cigarette nearly as much as the pipe smoke, and I thought to myself that when Grandmother lit her pipe next time, I would ask for a puff.

The fly fishing was good. We returned to the powwow with twenty-six speckled trout. Funny, I never thought of putting any back as I had when I caught the first great one years ago. I felt it was all right to take the fish because we needed them for food. Ella and Grandmother fried the fish in sweet corn oil; they were delicious, and reminded me of the soft-steamed fish of Kirabashi. I ate corn cakes until I literally could eat no more. The food at the powwow were all wonderful; the smoked venison was truly out of this world. We all had so much fun together. Charlie's grandpa looked older; his black hair was almost all white, and his braids were now two-toned, but he was still strong and healthy. He asked me all about Japan. He had no interest in Europe but his questions about the Japanese were endless: How did they speak? Were they friendly? Did they like Americans? How did they dress? What did they eat? Did I have friends there? I tried to answer all of them politely, but I grew somber when speaking of Tang and Madame Lee. Red Cloud put his big hand on my shoulder when he saw how it made me feel. "You love that place very much, don't you, little one?" he asked. I told him that indeed I did. It had felt just like this, like I was at home. "You know, the great spirit sometimes puts us in other places to remind us that we have knowledge of them. You must have been there in some other time and place in your journeying of the soul." He said, looking wise and old. When the Pow Wow came to its end, we went back to the lake, taking with us some of the smoked venison and fish.

Charlie came round on the Wednesday of that week to ask me to go fishing. I went happily. He was so very much older than I remembered, and so very handsome. We took Grandmother's rowboat and went out on the lake up to the north end, where the river runs into it. We fished most all day. Charlie and I talked and talked; we shared everything that had happened to each of us since we had last seen each other. The sun was beginning to go down when we decided that we had enough fish and should head for the dock. When we were unloading the fishing gear, Grandmother came down to help. She asked Charlie to stay for dinner and he accepted. He and I decided to go for a swim to cool off and get fresh for dinner. We raced to the mill pond and back; I nearly out-swam him. We climbed onto the dock laughing and suddenly, he kissed me right on the mouth, and before I could think, he had run off toward the house, yelling over his shoulder, "You're wonderful, you know!"

During dinner, I could feel the blood rush to my cheeks each time Charlie looked at me. We did the dishes for Grandmother afterward while she went out to smoke her pipe. "You didn't mind, did you? The . . . ah, kiss, I mean . . . I just felt like kissing you . . ." Charlie blurted out as we were finishing up. I thought about it a minute before I spoke, thinking that up till now I had only been kissed by women and male relatives. "No," I answered finally. "No, I didn't mind . . . I liked it." With that, I placed a kiss firmly on his cheek.

"Unah," he said. "Like this." He put his arms around me and kissed me like I had seen my father kiss Mother. It felt odd but very nice; I felt embarrassed and wonderful all at once. We walked out of the kitchen hand in hand to find Grandmother sitting on the steps, pipe in hand. To my surprise, she handed it to me. I took a little puff. The taste of the tobacco was as sweet as the smell. I passed it back to her; she smiled. "Sit down, children," she motioned to the steps. Charlie excused himself to go to his truck. He returned with the greatest pipe I had ever seen; it was carved out of red stone, its bowl was the face of a warrior. Charlie sat down on the other side of Grandmother and took out a leather pouch. I watched, fascinated, as he carefully filled and tapped the bowl of his pipe. When at last he lit it, the tobacco had a different smell, a woodsy smudge type scent like some of the ceremonial incense the Indians used. Charlie took a great puff, slowly letting the smoke roll out. Afterwards, he passed the pipe to Grandmother and then she passed it to me. The taste was wonderful; I loved the way it hung in my mouth and nose. We sat in silence until the pipe was finished. Charlie rose from the steps, "I've got to get back, and Pa will be worried that I'm not back with the truck." Grandmother told Charlie to come back soon. I walked him to his truck. He kissed me good night and told me that he was sure awful glad that I had come to spend the summer. I was, too. Life was suddenly new!

When I got back to the porch, Grandmother asked if I fancied a walk, so we went up toward the old mill. The moon was a full bright disk hanging in the sky like an ornament of some sort; the reflection in the pool was beautiful. We walked on for a ways in silence. "You are growing up, my real girl," Grandmother said after a while. "Soon you will be old enough to leave all of us behind, to go and make your own way in the world. Seeing you with Charlie makes me remember when I was your age. I married my husband the summer of my sixteenth year." I could tell that Grandmother wanted to say something important so I walked next to her in silence, only nodding my head now and then to let her know I was listening. She spoke of her life, the wonderful love that she and her husband had shared, of how the babies came and the wonder of each one filled their lives with even more love. She talked of the land and how they had built the house and the children had grown up there. She told me that at one time, there were two children in each of the five bedrooms and two in the attic room upstairs; how the depression came but they had plenty because of the garden; how the flu epidemic took her baby girl and the chickenpox took her middle boy; she told me the hows and whys of life in this quiet, simple place.

We turned and started to walk back toward the house as she finished. "You'll love a lot of young men along the way," she told me. "But be sure that the one you decide to marry is gentle, loving, and understanding. Don't ever let anyone force you to make a decision you will regret, and most of all, make sure that whoever you marry understands the keys of life: how to live simply, how to make fun out of natural things, how to speak with the earth, with G-d and with you. And most of all, be sure that he will love you without condition. Life is not perfect; each of us has our faults, but it's much easier to go on if there is someone beside us to share with and love, no matter what comes."

It was the deepest conversation I had ever had, and I knew that it was because Grandmother had seen Charlie kiss me. I felt that life was beginning a new turn for me, maybe that is why I had come here this summer. Next day, bright and early, Grandmother was up working in the garden. We had eaten a good breakfast of trout and eggs and I was carrying water back from the pump when I heard someone yell. At first, I thought it was Grandmother but as I set down the bucket, she came running toward me. "Where did the cry come from?" she asked, looking around. "Maybe the lake," I answered almost instantly. We both ran toward our dock. Out in the lake a ways, we could see an overturned row boat. I pushed our boat away from the dock and climbed in. Grandmother gave it one good shove and stepped in too, just as a second cry came. We rowed out as fast as we could to the overturned boat. There was a middle-aged man clinging to it. I dove into the water and helped him into our boat. "My dog . . ." the man stammered. I went around the overturned boat and thought I could hear something under it. Taking a great gulp of air, I dove down and came up beneath the boat. Sure enough, there was a black lab caught with a rope in the boat. He was managing to stay afloat because the boat had formed a small air pocket. I untied the rope and pulling it under with me, dragged the dog from beneath the boat. Grandmother and I managed to get the dog into our boat too. The man's right arm was broken and while Grandmother tried to assist him, I rowed us in to the shore. "Where did you come from?" Grandmother asked, trying to get information before the man was too shocked to answer. "I rented a small cabin on the edge of Gilman Creek," he answered weakly.

Once back at the ramp, we struggled to help the man onto the dock. The dog bounded out onto the shore and began to shake himself. "Your friend there is going to be just fine," Grandmother assured the man. "Leah, go on up to the house and call for the rescue team from up at the forest rangers to come. Tell them to hurry, I think he has broken some ribs besides his arm." I ran up to the house and did as Grandmother told me. On my way back, I grabbed a cup and filled it with warm tea from the pot, picked up a couple of blankets and ran back to where Grandmother sat with the man, who now looked pale and was shaking. We wrapped him in the blankets and let him sip the warm tea. His dog sat beside him, licking his face. After what seemed to be a long while, the rescue truck came. They put an IV in and put a splint on the arm, then they were ready to load him up. "What about Pat?" he asked weakly. The dog's tail wagged in response to the man's voice. "We'll look out for him until you can come get him," Grandmother answered. When the truck pulled out, I held Pat's collar so that he couldn't follow. He looked up at me with sad, knowing eyes. I patted his head and told him it would be okay, not to worry. After Grandmother and I both got cleaned up and into dry clothes, we sat in the kitchen sipping warm soup, with Pat, Blackie and Spot sitting by the door. "You acted very brave and grown up, diving in there. You made me so proud," Grandmother said. I felt very strange. I hadn't acted out of any thought but out of instinct. It was a new feeling that had not visited me before, a feeling that would come many times during my adult life. It was the sort of thing where, looking back, you have to wonder what it was that made you act so quickly without thought!

It turned out the gentleman we rescued was named Hank; he

was on vacation. He suffered several broken ribs and a fractured arm. When he came around four days later to fetch Pat, he brought Grandmother and me a big bouquet of roses and a thank-you card. "I can't tell you how many years I been fishing and never had anything happen. Boy, was I lucky that you two were within earshot. I could have died. Pat for sure would have," he told us. "We were glad to help," Grandmother and I replied.

Things were pretty calm for the rest of my stay. Charlie and I went fishing or swimming about every other day. I phoned Father in California to ask if he thought that I could go to school in the dells. He didn't like the idea and told me that he had thought about letting me go to South Dakota to live with my aunt and uncle there; they had a boy close to my age and would be happy to let me live with them for my senior year. Father also thought that the schools were better there than in California. I thought that would be all right, and so Father started to make the necessary arrangements.

The week before I was to leave the lake, Father flew out. Before he arrived, Grandmother had a real heart-to-heart talk with me. "Don't let your father know that I let you smoke, and for gosh sakes, don't let him see you with Charlie!" I laughed to myself, thinking about how free and easy Grandmother was about most of life, wondering where my Father got his stuffiness. I asked Grandmother about it and she said simply, "That's what a college degree did for him!" she laughed too.

Father and I had fun while he was there. I showed him how I'd learned to fly-fish and he laughed so hard he nearly overturned the boat. He was a real expert, so my version of the cast was really funny to him. But in the end, he had to admit that it worked, as I caught nearly twice as many fish. We had dinner with Charlie the last night before I had to leave. It was hard to think of going and I felt like I was losing my best friend. Charlie snuck in a kiss or too and when I walked him out to his truck, so did I. We promised to see each other next summer and to write at least once a week. I almost said "I love you," but something stopped me. Later, I would wish that I had.

Father and I took the train from Madison to Rapid City. I knew when I saw the pine trees that I was going to love it. The mountains rose off in the distance; dark, black outlines against a late August sky. Bright-colored leaves framed the outlines of the quiet city streets. The main street looked old-fashioned and there were few cars in the streets.

My Uncle Roy and Aunt Rose lived on a ranch where they raised beef cattle. They were kind, simple people who loved the idea of me staying with them. They had never had a girl and Aunt Rose quickly set about making me feel at home. She was a great seamstress; she could look at a picture and make things from it. The house was large. It had two large, stone fireplaces and knotty pine floors covered with hooked rugs in bright patterns that my Aunt had made. My room was in the loft of the second floor. It had its own bathroom and from my windows I could see the Black Hills. I fell in love at first sight!

My cousin Jimmy wasn't a real nice young man; he was rough around the edges and lacked manners, but I decided that before the year was over, I would make him like me! Father stayed long enough to get me into school and well settled. He left on Labor Day weekend, headed back to California and then on to Guam where he had been assigned as a special envoy to one of the generals in charge of the Vietnam Offensive. Already, I had heard enough about Vietnam to think that we shouldn't be involved there, so I was worried that Father had been given such an assignment. This fact coupled with my outspokenness had already gotten me into one argument with Jimmy, and doubtless it would get me into more.

Against his father's wishes, Jimmy was trying to enlist in the Marines because, as he put it, "At least this way I get to choose my own team, and I don't have to get drafted!" The whole idea frightened me in a way I had never been frightened before. The newspapers were full of how many of our young men had already signed up or been drafted. What it didn't say was that we were already losing young men by the hundreds who had no business in harm's way. War was supposed to be for a reason; it was supposed to have a purpose, the way the Second World War had. It was supposed to be because there was an evil injustice in the world that had to be stopped. But to me, Vietnam already seemed without reason. I couldn't imagine why Jimmy would want to enlist, even if he would get drafted. I told Jimmy that I thought he should just wait and see. "They won't draft you while you're in school. Be patient!" He glared at me. "I'm in college! They can draft me anytime they choose! I just want some choice as to how I go."

I couldn't understand; it all seemed unfair. How could our government be doing such things? I wrote to Father, demanding an explanation. He wrote back and told me not to "bother my pretty head about it." I was even angrier. Father was the one person I had always relied on for straight answers in my life.

Then the worst possible thing happened: Charlie wrote that he had received his draft notice. He would be leaving for boot camp in California. Suddenly, I hated being home. The States seemed foreign to me and the war seemed all too close. Suddenly, I was sorry that I hadn't told him that I loved him!

Chapter XVIII

Whatever I lacked in the way of being a young lady, I made up for with my intelligence. High school was fun, but I didn't relate well to other girls. I just couldn't seem to get the hang of being in a click. Aunt Rose was great!

Much like Grandmother when I would come home with a tale of another failed attempt at fitting in, she would look at me with her pretty, doe-brown eyes and say, "Don't worry dear, they are not as educated about the world as you. And besides, they aren't half as smart!" Then we would go down to the Walgreen's and get a malt together, or sometimes we would just go out horseback riding.

I stuck out in class like a sore thumb. One of my English teachers even thought that I cheated on a test because I got an A when he had bragged that "No One will get a perfect score!" He went so far as to call my aunt to warn her of his suspicions. What he didn't know was that our family stuck up for each other. Monday morning after the call, my aunt drove me to school and filed a formal complain with the principal about the call. Suddenly I found myself in a different English class, one where the teacher had traveled extensively with her military husband!

I began to read about our government, about our involvement in the first and second world wars, then Korea and now, this mess in Vietnam. I was trying hard to make myself believe we should be there and that it was all right for a young man like Charlie or Jimmy to be drafted into the service against their wishes.

In my U.S. History class, I was the pride of the teacher. Mr. Wallis loved me; he said I was "insightful," and that I had a way of looking at things that was "totally refreshing." One afternoon, I went up to his office on the third floor to talk with him about the war. He didn't tell me to not "bother my pretty head about it." To my surprise, he asked me to sit down. We had a long discussion about the whole Vietnam thing. When it was over, I realized that it was an economical issue for our country, that not all adults felt it was all right, and that Mr. Wallis was as angry as I was because his oldest son was over there.

I wrote a paper for my Literature class; it was an exposé on the removal of the Creek and the Cherokee Indians from their lands by the government. While I was researching the paper, I found a lot of stories that told me that here was another time in our history when young soldiers had been forced to do things that went against their moral, religious, and personal beliefs. The anger inside of me grew.

I talked a lot about things with Aunt Rose. She was patient and kind. She was also a devoted American. One day, over our malts, she tried to explain that we Americans only get involved when we feel we have a duty to the rest of the world because things are so good here. I told her that I didn't think Vietnam was that sort of case. She listened intently; she even asked if she could read some of the stuff that I was studying. And she did! One afternoon about a week later, we were told that we would be let out of school early because the League of Women Voters of the county were going to stage a march for Peace in Vietnam. I went downtown with some of my friends to watch. There was my Aunt Rose. I could hardly believe my eyes. When she spotted me standing on the steps at the library, she came out of the march and grabbed me, taking me back in with her. "Sweetheart, you are right! I've been talking with these women all week; we have to begin to voice our opinions!" I was so proud I marched the whole way to the draft board headquarters with them. It was the first of many such marches that I would participate in.

Life was steady ups and downs at school. Some of my teachers loved my intelligence, some hated it. But one thing is for sure, it separated me from the rest of the kids. I had friends among the Indians and the few blacks, but not any real friends among the whites. The other girls snubbed me. I dated a friend of Jimmy's for a while, and then one of the school football squad took a liking to me because I said in assembly one Friday that I didn't think it was right for our young men to be in Vietnam!

Brad was a quarterback. He was worried that he would graduate in the spring and be snatched up by the draft. He wasn't real smart, but he had lived overseas because his dad was an Air Force pilot. He and his family lived at Ellsworth Air force Base outside of town. We had fun together and it made me forget about the fact that, try as I would, I couldn't seem to fit in with the rest of the crowd. He had a little red American Rambler. We went to the football games together and often went to the dances. He had an older brother who was at the School of Mines and Technology. Todd was a handsome, blond young man. One morning when Brad picked me up for school, he looked upset. When I asked what was wrong, he told me that Todd had been drafted. I was so angry I cried. Brad and I went to talk with Mr. Wallis. We wanted more than anything to do something. He told us that we could write to our congressmen or even to the President, but that it was probably not going to stop things.

For the first time, I felt totally helpless. Grandmother always said that you can make changes in almost everything if you try. I wanted to believe that was true but deep down, I knew that it wasn't. I decided that I had to start meditating again. I was so emotional about the War. The same day that I found a spot near an old willow on Uncle Roy's land, Jimmy got his draft notice.

At dinner that night, we were all sad. Uncle Roy said simply that Jimmy had to do his duty for G-d and Country. Jimmy glared and wouldn't eat. He said, "If I had only enlisted, I would feel better." I felt like yelling at someone and my dear Aunt Rose sat dabbing her eyes with her pretty calico apron. Next day, I went to the library. I asked the reference clerk to show me the federal laws about drafting. I pored over them for days on end, struggling through the legal garble, trying to make what they said sound true. Then I stumbled onto something. There was an article that stated that if a son was your only son, you could petition to have him exempted from the draft!

I ran all the way home. "Aunt Rose, Jimmy doesn't have to go!" I shouted. "He can be exempted!" She came out of the sewing room, needle still in hand. "What do you mean . . . exempted?" she asked, looking at me incredulously.

"Come to the library with me, please," I pleaded. Without a second thought, she laid down the needle, took off her little half glasses and her apron, grabbed her purse and followed me out the door. "Let's drive there," she said, heading round the garage.

I took her to the exact place where I had found the item in the law book. She read it over and over, then she asked the librarian if she would please make us a copy. We drove home, me re-reading it out loud to her. "I think you're right," she said as we drove into the driveway.

Jimmy was in the kitchen drinking a glass of milk when we walked in. "Look," his mother said, shoving the copy at him. He took it and began to read. He read it again. "Does it mean I don't have to comply?" he asked, looking at the two of us. "That's what it means," I said. "It means we can apply to have you be exempted because you are their only son!" Jimmy flew at me. He grabbed me round the waist and boosted me up in the air. "You are something!" he said. "Really something! You are just so damned smart!"

I had no idea what chain of events my discovery would set off. Next day, I came home to find a dozen ladies in the living room of our house. One of them was a lawyer friend of Aunt Rose. They were poring over a bunch of law books, taking notes and all seemingly talking at once. One of the ladies I knew well, she was Brad's mom, looked up as I popped my head in. She got right up and came over to the entryway. "Ladies, this is Elizabeth. She is the one we have to thank for finding this out!" Suddenly, I was surrounded with chattering women. When I finally broke myself free, I rushed up to my room.

Life in this sleepy little town would never quite be the same. Every family in town who had an only son was soon visiting our house. They came in droves from way out in the country, from the reservation, even up from the one small town out in the Badlands. I came home one afternoon to TV cameras and news people. South Dakota was on the move. The League of Women Voters had activated a lobby group; they were going to Washington and Aunt Rose was going with them. Jimmy received a notice from the draft that he was now exempt. They gave him a number – and he brought me flowers!!! I hugged him tight and he whispered, "Too bad you are my cousin; you are my kind of girl!"

Suddenly lots of the guys at school thought I was a hero. Someone put my name in the Winter Ball Queen entries, and even though I had not been very popular or accepted before, I was now! Girls that wouldn't give me the time of day for the last three months suddenly bragged that they were my "best friends." I kept to myself as much as I could. I didn't enjoy the notoriety, but having some girls ask me to Walgreen's after school was nice. I didn't really believe that they liked me. In fact, I knew that the truth was their parents thought that I was terrific so they had to act as if they liked me. But still, it was nice.

Mr. Wallis applauded me for my sheer tenacity. "Who else would have thought to go searching through the rules? You were the only one. I'm a teacher and I didn't think about it. We all just followed along like sheep with our heads in the sand!" Mr. Duckworth, the principal, referred to me as an anti-American who just loved to stir up trouble. My Aunt Rose made him apologize in front of school assembly. My literature teacher gave me an assignment to put the "No Only Sons" story into a format for the school paper. I did and to my surprise, they printed it and next day it appeared in the city newspaper. My grandmother wrote to me about what I was doing. She loved it. "My real girl," she said. "You keep this up and your daddy will disown you!" My Tante Rivka cheered me on by phone. "Truth is Important," she said. "More important that anything else in life!"

My father was silent: no letters, no phone calls. My weekly allowance arrived in a plain envelope without even a note. Aunt Rose said, "Never mind," Jimmy said. "It's okay, lil' sis . . . I love you!" I worried. Was it right for me to be so outspoken? Should I have been silent like everyone else?

School was good; I had a 4.0 average and several universities had already sent me invitations to entertain their campuses as my college choice. I read about all the different universities but most of all, I wanted to go to music school, not just any music school but Juilliard in New York! I knew in my heart that Father would never approve of such a choice, and so I began to seriously consider what other college I might like. It was already January by the time that I had made my choice. I decided to go to Berkeley in northern California. Why, I'm not sure now, looking back. But I felt that the school lent itself to intellectualism and more importantly, that it allowed for more individual freedom in the curriculum as well as in the university life.

That month I got my last letter from Charlie. I remember that I walked out to the willow tree to read it. The air was bitterly cold; my breath nearly froze in front of me. The landscape was still hidden under the deep winter snow. "I wish that I could be back home," he wrote. "It is terrible here; everyday, I see things that are too ugly to write about. I feel afraid even in my sleep." Three days later, Grandmother would call to say that he had been killed in action. I mourned in the Japanese fashion; first, I cried my eyes out in silence, bent over my knees on the mat that I had carried from Kirabashi. Then I went out and found Jimmy and asked him to take me for a soda. On the way, I explained how Tang's family had celebrated so he decided we'd get a picnic together the next day and go out to the far end of the ranch and set off fireworks. We did, and I thanked Jimmy for being there. It felt right. It made saying goodbye to my first love easier. Jimmy had brought along a surprise: it was a miniature flag. We set it in the snow next to a picture of Charlie, like a memorial tablet. It stuck in my mind for a long while that Charlie wouldn't have needed to go if I had found the rule about only sons sooner!

Father finally wrote to me. He said he was sorry about my friend and that he wished life didn't have to come with wars, but that it just did. He said that Charlie had died in the service of his country and that was a proud, wonderful thing. I didn't write back. I couldn't accept that dying a death for a cause that no one understood was honorable .My political self was beginning to take form. I was decidedly against our involvement in Vietnam. I was also decidedly against any sort of draft. It seemed that there were a lot of young people and mothers who thought the same way I did. I had continued my piano lessons with a nice Englishwoman named Mrs. Wellington while there. I played with the high school orchestra for concerts and sometimes, I sang. Spring was coming and there was a talent show to be given in the auditorium of the school. I worked with Brad on a skit; it was to be a spoof about the senselessness of prejudice and war.

The day we auditioned, the drama teacher, Mrs. Sharp, told us we did a fine job but that she couldn't use us because of the political content. She suggested that we rewrite the skit to put it in a different time of our country's history. We did; we called it *Uncle Macaroni goes to Richmond*. It was great! The night of the performance, we received a standing ovation. We didn't win first prize but we got a point across!

I wasn't happy with the silence between Father and me. I talked about it with Aunt Rose and she said that everyone goes through tough times with parents while they are becoming adults, but it bothered me a lot. I wrote to Mother, something that I hadn't done in a long time. To my surprise, she wrote back. It was only a short note. "Don't get so involved in political issues," she said. "In the end of things, it will only end up hurting you and everyone around you." I thought about what she wrote and I knew in the heart of me that she was right. I just couldn't seem to stop myself, though, so I went on being outspoken and voicing my opinions about the war.

Spring brought change to the countryside; the snow melted and everything began to turn lush and green. Crocuses' heads peeked out of the little bits of leftover snow down the hillside, robins appeared at the bird feeder on the fence, and graduation was just around the bend. I would turn seventeen on the sixteenth of April and graduate from high school, Magna Cum Laude on the fifth of June.

I wanted to go see Grandmother in the summer, but my heart ached that I would not be seeing Charlie. The image of the lake without him seemed dull. Mother refused to come for my graduation but Aunt Rose made up for it in many ways. She made me a beautiful gown for my prom: it was a sea-foam, green toile with a peacock head on the shoulder sewn out of sequins and beads. Down my back cascaded his tail. It was elegant. Brad took me to the prom. We had a great time. After the traditional breakfast the next morning, we all climbed into dungarees and went up to the State Park. We drank all day and by evening were so sloshed that we forgot to go home. A bunch of our parents came to get us. I was in trouble with Uncle Roy but Aunt Rose took care of my hangover and said she understood completely!

Graduation day dawned bright and beautiful. I received my degree and several honors, including the Citizen Activist Award from the League of Women Voters. I was sorry that I would be leaving Aunt Rose, Jimmy and Uncle Roy. Sorry too that I would be leaving the lovely Black Hills. I had grown to love the place even though times had been tough, from a social point of view. Next Saturday morning when they took me to the train, Jimmy said, "You ever need anything, lil' sis, you just call me and I'll be right there." I laughed and made some remark about the lyrics from a song, while deep down thinking, "For a kid who didn't like anything including himself when I arrived nine months earlier, he had grown a lot." He was now the head of a "No First Sons" group and traveled all around making sure that everyone knew "the true facts," as he put it. He hugged me real tight when

I was boarding the train. I loved him too, I realized. The train pulled slowly out of the depot. I watched the distance grow between us. Uncle Roy, Aunt Rose and Jimmy stood on the ramp watching until I couldn't see them anymore. I bowed my head into my lap and cried. Was life always saying goodbye? I wondered. Does a person ever come to a place that is finally home?

≽ Chapter XIX

The train ride seemed long. The countryside slipped by as if in a dream. Finally, I arrived at my destination. I sat there in my seat until nearly all the passengers had left. Finally, I gathered my coat and bag and eased my way down the aisle and out the door. Grandmother and Uncle Lloyd stood on the ramp, waiting for me. I couldn't help myself; I started to cry again. This was the only place that was always there for me, this magical, wonderful place where those who loved me were always waiting. Grandmother held out her arms to me and I sank into them, grateful to be there once more.

We drove straight to the reservation to see Red Cloud and Ella. They took me to the spot where they had made a resting place for the ashes of Charlie. I cried some more . . . Finally, Ella said: "Enough, child. You'll be sick. He wouldn't want that. He loved you and would be proud that you stood here today. There wasn't a thing he would have changed even if he could . . . life is just like that. One day you'll know that there are some things written in the stone of our lives that neither we nor anyone else can change. We must just walk the path as best we can. We must carry on and never look back!" I walked down the little path from the cemetery between Ella and Grandmother. I knew that Ella was right and I vowed that I would never be silent about injustice no matter what that would cost me.

It was good to reach the house. Seeing the door, getting the greeting from the dogs all made me breathe easier. As soon as I had changed clothes, I took a long walk out to the great rocks where once I had seen the eagle eye to eye. Carefully, I climbed up to the top, to the perch where I had sat so often before. I sat cross-legged there, watching the sky turn to the golden hues of sunset. Just as the last golden rays of light bounced across the lake's surface, I saw him. He came flying right at me as if I wasn't there, a great eagle with wings at least six feet across. The air from them brushed my face, and a most amazing thing happened; he landed. He was not more than three feet from me, looking at me with great golden eyes. He turned his head slowly from side to side, made one great call that rang back and forth among the rocks and was gone! Years later, looking back on that moment, I remember that I felt like I was seeing an old friend . . . maybe even Charlie.

I tried to relate the incident to Grandmother, but she halted me in mid-stream. "There are some things in this universe of ours we are never supposed to share, some things that happen just for us, that are meant to soothe us and to give us courage. This is one of those things." I decided she was right. I stored the image in my heart and it has lived there ever since. I can tell you that I have visited it many times when I was in need of courage and strength beyond my own ability, and it has always given me just what I needed.

I welcomed the quiet, restful days at the lake. There was no news of Vietnam here to invade my meditation. It was wonderful how the old house stayed the same. Grandmother, as always, seemed not to have changed. I wondered how even her hair seemed to remain much as when I first saw her; everyone else changed. Ella was so old that her skin had taken on the appearance of a wrinkled, tan, apple doll, the kind made with a face carved out of an apple and then dried; and Red Cloud, whose hair was all white now, looked like an image from the past, leathery and fine with such wisdom that it astounded you just to look at him.

The dogs had aged: Blackie had white hair all around his muzzle now; Spot limped in the early mornings when he first woke. But they were still playful and loved to swim with me. I spent a lot of time alone. Grandmother fretted and said that I should go into the dells and see some of the people I knew, so at last I went to see Sadie. She was living in the guest home of her daughter-in-law now. She was glad to have a visitor but I don't think that she recognized me, not until I said, "Do you remember what you told me? That I should be my mother's memory?" It was like a key turning a great lock; she came to herself and began to talk about the camps and I sat with her the rest of the day, only leaving when she fell asleep.

I tried to focus to get myself prepared for college. I went down to Madison and went shopping for clothes. I got my hair cut. For most of my life, it had been long enough to braid or put up in a bun. I picked out a pretty, short style that would be easy to care for with my curls. I had the girl braid my hair in one long braid and then cut it off and tied the piece so that I could send it to Mother. I knew that she would be upset by my short hair and thought that maybe if she had the braid, she wouldn't care as much.

When I arrived back at the house, Grandmother squealed. "Oh, my real girl, what have you done?" I promised her that she would get used to it, it would grow on her but I didn't think she was convinced. I, on the other hand, loved it after years of wearing old-fashioned hairdos and envying the other girls and their modern styles. I felt great! When I looked in the mirror, the face looking back looked grown up, and even pretty. I experimented with makeup and found that what I liked best was very easy eye color with mascara and just a very light bit of cream makeup, with a fair blush that was hardly noticeable. I guess I was getting ready for California. My father had sent me a subscription to *Seventeen* magazine while I was with Aunt Rose and I took most of my ideas from there. It was fun! I thought that living in a dorm and being on my own was going to be great!

The month at the lake was over too soon. I had just began to feel like my old self again, had a set schedule of meditation and had been happy about life in general for that last couple of weeks. There was no choice, however. I had to be home to San Francisco to get everything signed and ready for school. In fact, I had to be on campus at Berkeley by the 21st of August.

Grandmother and Uncle Lloyd drove me into Madison to the airport. I loved flying so I considered this a real treat. It would be the first time that I would fly without my father. Grandmother held me tight when they announced my boarding call. She whispered, "No matter where you are, just think of me waiting here for you. You can call twice a month and I'll pay for it!" I held her tight in my arms, smelling deeply the scent of this one special person in my life, the one who never changed, who had always loved me unconditionally since the first moment she saw me.

The flight was nice; we made one stop in Denver, which was a bit rough on both landing and taking off but otherwise I loved it. We flew over the clouds much of the way until just before landing in San Francisco. When the pilot announced that we would be beginning our descent and we came down under the canopy, the sight took my breath away. We were out over the water and below us were sailboats and big ships, going to and fro under the arch of the bridge. Off in the distance, there were trees and hills. When we made our final turn, the city lay ahead of us; it was spectacular. Again, I thought that one day I would like to learn to fly.

Mother and Ann were waiting in the terminal. This time, I could have walked past both of them without them noticing. I felt that it was incredulous; my own mother didn't recognize me. I walked up to her and said, "Hello, Mother!" She took one look at me and turned pale as a ghost. "Leah, is it truly you?" she stammered. "Truly, it is you . . . you look just like Rivka when we were young." I had chosen to wear a hat; it was a bouncy little barrette type of thing and at first she didn't notice that I had cut my hair. Just as well, I thought to myself. She might faint if she saw it right now. I kept the hat on, deciding that I would not take it off until we were home. Ann gave me one of her usual hearty hugs. I thought, "Another person who seems not to change!"

We gathered my luggage with the help of a skycap and were quickly on our way. The streets of the city when we reached them were so busy; it made me fell breathless in the same way that Tokyo had. We didn't talk much on the way. Ann told me that Father would be in on Wednesday night and we would go to pick him up together at the military field. Mother volunteered that there had been some changes at the house since I was last there, but that was all just small talk.

Finally arriving, I noticed that the yard out front now sported two olive trees as well as the original weeping willow and was very sculptured and clean-looking. I was shocked when I entered the front doors. Mother had replaced the entryway floor and it was now made of gray-tan tiles that made clicking noises when you crossed it. Upstairs, my room sported the same carpet, but now the wallpaper was covered with green ivy and the curtains were navy blue. Ugh, I thought. I was very busy looking and I thought to myself, "If I ever have a home of my own, I'm never going to have wall paper, and certainly will never pick dark drapes with dark carpet!"

I freshened my makeup, combed my hair, picked up the box that held my braid, and started downstairs. Ann met me on the way. "Look at you! You've turned into a real beauty! You look like one of those girls in the fashion magazines! And look at your hair! You've bobbed it! You have!" She smiled and straightened one of the unruly curls at the side of my cheek. "I like this look!" she said, and walked on up the stairs.

I found Mother sitting with a cup of tea in the living room. It had changed completely; the carpet was a soft yellow, which was reflected in the stripped wall paper as well as the under-curtains at the draped windows. The chairs and couch I didn't recognize. They were done in an Oriental pattern that was, to my surprise, quite pleasing. All in all, I liked the feel of the whole room. My mother's back was to me; she was sitting in a wing chair which faced a window on the backyard. Beyond her I could see a lovely garden with roses everywhere and out at the far end, a small gazebo framed a bench. That too seemed lovely.

She heard me after a second or two. "You may come in, and I have tea for us," she said, as if speaking to a stranger. I walked over and stood by her chair. She didn't look up right away. "Mother, I've cut my hair." I said it matter-of-factly just to get it out of the way. "You what?" she asked, finally looking up at me. "Oh my! What will you do when you get married? You're supposed to have it cut when you get married . . . or is that too old fashioned?" she asked almost apologetically. "Here," I replied, shoving the box at her that held my braid. "Here, it's in here." Her face blanched white. She put her hand to her cheek but she took the box. "I guess I should be grateful that you saved it," she said, half questioning, half statement. "Put it somewhere, dear, and sit down. Your tea will be cold." I couldn't believe she hadn't fainted. She always fainted when things didn't please her. I sat down, stunned, and picked up my teacup, feeling as if I might faint myself.

We sat there sipping tea. She told me all about the wonderful Japanese gardener she had found and how he had made everything look "grand." She shared that Father had redone the living room just last fall before he left. He had picked an Oriental interior designer. Did I like it? The afternoon passed pleasantly enough. I was surprised. It was as if we were on different terms. Was it she who had changed? Or I? I wondered.

We went out for dinner. Mother said it was because she hardly ever did and she thought it would be fun, just us girls. We went to a Russian restaurant downtown. It was elegantly decorated. The music was live and the food was amazingly wonderful. We chatted like two friends. She asked about Japan and how I came to love it so much. She even asked about South Dakota. "Your father was quite upset with you, all that political thing, but it reminded me of when I was your age in Russia. The Great Revolution had come and we were full of ourselves; we thought that we were on top of the world. I was quiet and shy but your Tante Rivka . . . she was involved with everything. Mother would tell her that it was not good. She would laugh and call Mother old-fashioned."

The evening went by quickly. We talked until after midnight there in the Russian restaurant, sipping red Russian tea and tiny, straight-sided glasses of sweet vodka. I felt as if, for the first time, we were really communicating. She said not one bad thing to me; she even forced me to get up and dance when a young man who was sitting at a table across from us asked me. She danced with his father. It was all unreal to me.

Later that night I would sit on my mat trying to meditate, to quiet myself so that I could fall asleep. I couldn't help wondering where this side of her had been when I was small. She was fun; she laughed, she danced, she chattered away like I was a wonderful friend. Finally, I was able to crawl into bed and sleep. That night I dreamed about the eagle. He flew right at me again. In the morning when I awoke, I found a vase of roses sitting by my bed with a little note card that said, "When you wake up, find me in the garden and we'll have breakfast."

I showered, did my hair and makeup, dressed in a summer dress and went downstairs and out into the rose garden. She was there with a great sunhat on, gloves covering her hands, clipping roses. "Good morning, liepschen!" she called, coming up the path. She kissed me . . . on my cheek! I stammered, I'm sure, as I said "Good morning." "I'm hungry, are you?" she asked heading for the back door which led into the kitchen. "Today Ann has to go to the Doctor, so I'll fix us some blintzes," she said, washing her hands at the sink. "I'd like to learn how to do that," I said, half expecting that she would say no. "Well, get out the eggs and the cream while I measure the flour and spices. Let's have you learn." I nearly fell over; she was really nice! Why all those years had she always been so cold? What was the difference? Was it because I was older and didn't need to have her care? Or was it because I had changed, because I had learned that love and nurturing could be found in other places?

We actually had fun. She laughed at me when I fumbled trying to turn the delicate pastries, then showed me her secret. "You put a bit of butter on the end of the spatula so that it won't stick." We ate blintzes with cream-cheese filling, smothered in smooth raspberry jam. We cleaned up the kitchen so that, as Mother put it, "Ann won't be upset with the mess." We went back out and she showed me where to pick a rose so that a new bud would form on the stem. I was amazed!

The three days between my arrival and Father's was a whirl of nice activity and for the very first time, I heard Mother talk about some of the things that had happened in her young life. The night before he was due home, we went out to dinner again. This time, to a Jewish Deli. We had a great time. Mother ordered for us in Yiddish. We had corned beef, knishes and cabbage. It was great! When we got home, she actually hugged me good night. I wanted to ask her so many things but I didn't want to break the spell. It was good to be home; I didn't want to do anything to upset the flow.

The night Father was to arrive, Mother surprised Ann and I with wanting to go to the airport too. She said "It wouldn't seem right staying home." We arrived at the terminal just as Father's plane began to unload. I spotted him coming down the steps and ran to the gate to meet him. I waved my arms so he would see me. At first, he didn't wave back and then he was sprinting toward us. He looked like a soldier!

He gave me a quick squeeze then picked Mother right off her feet and kissed her hard as she held onto her hat. When at last he put her back on the ground, she was smiling all over. He took a moment on the spot to look at me. He made me take off my hat and turn around. "You are right," he said to Mother. "She looks just like Rivka." The drive home was full of catching up. Father wanted to know if the living room had turned out as he planned;, how were the roses and the dogs. The conversation never came round my way and I felt a tinge of jealousy, but I knew that was how it was between them. They both adored each other for all their faults.

Ann and I unloaded the car back at the house. Father and Mother disappeared upstairs and that was the last we saw of them until morning. Ann made coffee and she and I drank our way through the pot while I shared with her all that had been happening with Mother and I. She told me that she thought Mother felt relieved now that I was older; that maybe she hadn't been a good mother, but maybe now we could be friends. I told Ann then about Tante Rivka. She sat staring at me for a long while. "I always knew there was some secret," she told me. "Something more to the way things were than we knew. I hope that somehow you find a way to mend it all . . . the pain, I mean, and the neglect, or maybe you have already." I shared with her about Kirabashi, Tang, Madame Lee, and about Aunt Rose. "I think I found my own way, without her loving me," I said at last. "Maybe I am actually a better person because she didn't." When I went up to my bed that night, I passed Mother's room. I could hear Father and her talking softly to one another. I fell asleep thinking of Kirabashi.

⌦ Chapter XX

Life was suddenly sweet again. I loved being with Father and realized that I had missed him. He and I had a special bond that gave us wonderful times. We went out to Berkley on the first Saturday after he arrived home. It was what I had pictured and more. The old bell tower sounded just as we pulled into the Commons parking lot. I got to tour my dorm, see the room I would share with one other girl, and meet the dorm mother. She struck me as out of date. She appeared in the hall after a tap on her door, wearing a pair of fluffy pink house slippers and a robe. It was already two o'clock in the afternoon! I giggled; Father glared!

The campus impressed me. The dorm room didn't but I went away with a list of things that I could bring that would make it better. The air of the campus was one of a place in flux. There were a few anti-Vietnam posters on some of the kiosks, and a banner left over from a protest hung over the quad. I liked it. Father gave me a long lecture about the evils of getting involved in campus politics, or politics at all, for that matter. The lecture lasted the whole way back to the house. He didn't come right out and confront the things I had been into last year at high school but he slammed me for being against anything that our government sanctioned, ending just as we drove into the drive with, "Let me tell you, I have a plan if you do get involved again. You won't like it but I'll take extreme measures if you embarrass me again, as you did with the "No Only Sons" stint!"

For the first time in my life, I didn't agree with Father. "You have no right to tell me not to think. You have worked with government all your life. Maybe, just maybe, you are too close to the forest to see the trees," I told him. "Why do you think that you are the only one who could possibly be right? I found a rule that the government set in place to protect families from losing their only sons. It wasn't wrong to make sure that people are aware. If it is, then this country isn't free and democracy is a lie!"

He didn't say a word, not then and not for the rest of the evening. We sat through dinner with Mother and I trying to converse, and him glaring. When he excused himself to go have a brandy, Mother moved into his chair and started to talk with me about it. "You have a right to your own mind, I truly believe that, and you also have a duty to tell what you know to be the truth. War is ugly, and the horror of it is unspeakable. You weren't wrong. I never agreed with Rivka but now, looking back, I think to myself, "At least she did something." When we knew that the Nazis were coming, she wanted to run with our children, to run away even though neither of our husbands thought that we needed to. She was right! In the camp, she was strong. She was never too afraid to steal from the guards, and she did. We probably survived just on her strength, her ability to see a way around things. You are very much like her. I know that you are only going to do things that you think will make a difference. Don't let your father dissuade you from your ideals; don't let him push you into blindness. I haven't the heart to defend you in front of him, but I wanted to let you know that whatever you do, it's all right! Be brave and don't ever give up your ideals. Don't let the government strip you of your personality. Don't let them take from you what G-d has given you. Believe that you are right! I'll speak with your father. I can't promise that it will change anything, but I will speak with him!"

With that, Mother rose from the table, patted my hand and left the room. "I wished that I had a pipe, I'd go out to the gazebo and have a smoke," I thought as I walked out into the kitchen to try to find Ann. I felt as if my father and I had declared war on each other that day and oddly, for the first time, I felt that Mother was firmly on my side and actually would defend me from him if she had to.

I guess that the difference between Mother and I had somehow softened because I was getting more mature, but maybe too because somehow, she saw the struggle going on in our country and it reminded her of her own country all those years before. Later that night, there was TV news about a protest at a draft center in the Midwest somewhere. Mother shook her head and said, "Ach! Shades of Nazi Germany!" and left the room. Father got up and turned off the TV. "Nonsense!" he said, and went into his study and closed the door.

I went up to my room. I mulled over the papers from Berkley; I thought about what I could do to make the old ugly dorm room look nicer. It would take a miracle! I thought. I read a bit of Gandhi's *Treatise on Non-Violent Protest* and fell asleep. Next morning when I awoke Father was packing his bags; he had been called back to Washington on some business, he said. Mother looked pale and nodded for me to leave them alone. I went to the kitchen and got a cup of coffee. Ann was on the back patio and I joined her. It was going to be warm, I could tell from the smell. "Your father is angry with you," she said. "I know," was all I could answer. "It's the way of things when you get about grown up," Ann started. "I recall how my father was because I wanted to join the girls who worked in the airplane factory during the war. He thought I'd be ruined for life, doing a man's job. I went right on ahead and took a job as a rivet fitter. I loved it, and Dad never forgave me for doing what I thought was right. It was my own effort to help the war. They needed us girls to replace the men who had gone overseas. Eventually, I even learned to fly a plane and would help to move them across the country. My dad never knew that I did. Mother and I would concoct some story or other about a friend being ill and off I'd go. When Dad died, he told me that I was the reason for every gray hair on his head. I expect you're going to give your father a few." "Remember, Ann . . . He is after all my stepfather!" I said. It was out of my mouth before I knew it. There was a division, and I blamed it on his not being my real father. I truly felt that if he were my real father, he would understand.

Mother came out to the patio and asked that I come in and tell Father goodbye. I went, but not the way I had many times before. I could feel the ice like a great wall between us. "You take care of your paperwork for school, and have your mother help you get whatever you need for that dorm room. I'll be back mid-week, just before you have to be on campus." I hugged him, and that was that. First time in my life that I ever felt a distance from him

Mother took me to brunch down at the Russian Tea Room. We talked about what I should do. She never once suggested that I back down or even apologize for my activity back in Rapid. "Be patient, my dear," she said. "He'll be better once he knows where he is going next, or if in fact he is going." "What do you mean 'if'?" I asked her.

Mother explained that Father had complained a lot while he was in Guam, and that she thought he might be ready to stay home. She shared with me that he had written that it was difficult seeing so many wounded boys with only half of themselves left, coming through Guam on the way home. We worked through the week and found some nice things for my dorm room. I got a sunny, yellow-and-green comforter and pillow sham, a neat clock-radio that came on as an alarm, an Oriental-looking reading light and a small but very pretty rug that was washable, for beside my bed.

Mother went with me to buy some clothes too. We had fun. She actually got the idea of what I liked and could roam among the racks, coming back to the dressing room with things I might have picked myself. One afternoon, we were having a soda and I asked, "Didn't you like babies?" She hesitated and smiled softly. "I did, really I did. I loved my babies when they came. You were different. It wasn't easy there in New York; I was alone and I was never brave like Rivka."

I tried to get her to go on but she stopped there. Somehow it was all just too painful for her, I could see that and even had empathy for it. I was enjoying her so much that I was hesitant to ruin any of our time so I let it go at that. Father returned on the Friday before I was due to go to campus. He looked happy and announced to Mother that he would be working in the embassy building in San Francisco. She was delighted. "At last!" she sighed.

He still didn't speak to me unless it was necessary. I felt unhappy, confused, and most of all, hurt. I decided that we needed to clear the air so after dinner, when we had a moment, I asked him if he would try to understand, try to see things from my perspective. "I can, and I do," he answered. "But the government is always right. What we have, how we live is because I know what to say, what to leave unsaid and how to follow the command of our government. Maybe in private I don't always agree, but I would never do anything in public that would be offensive. That's all I'm trying to say to you. Think what you want; say what you want in the privacy of our home, but not in public, not where the news people will repeat it. I just don't want you to go up to campus on Monday and join some crusade, because I know you have that in you. It's a part of your very being. I hope you will be more particular about what you get wrapped up in there in college."

Suddenly, I saw an entirely different side of Father, a side that was not quite open, truthful, and honest. Was this that part of him that I had sensed sometime in the past and not liked? I couldn't help but wonder to myself.

Monday came swiftly. Father and Mother drove me up so that they could help me get my things settled in the dorm. The campus was full of people: parents bringing students, airport shuttles dropping off students. It was one huge mess. We arrived at my assigned dorm, signed the necessary papers, and I took Mother up to my room while Father went to ferry the things from the parking lot to the dorm. When I opened the door to my room, Mother gasped! I had thought it looked ugly and rather old but this confirmed it! Someone had rolled the mattresses up on the beds and done a semi-cleaning job, but it still had the dusty smell of an old house. Mother took off her gloves and sat down in the desk chair. "We will need cleaning things; we'll have to send your father to a store." She sat there a moment more and then rose and opened both of the windows. Just about then, a young girl in blue jeans and a hippie vest over a white blouse appeared at the door. "Ugh!" she stated. "We need a mom!"

My mother turned and in her best fashion said, "Hello, I'm Leah's mom. Don't worry, I'll stay till we get it clean for you." "I'm Charlotte," the girl offered. "I am glad you are here! This looks worse than I expected. I thought it would be more . . . well . . . modern, this being California and all."

I knew at once that Charlotte was from the South; her southern drawl rolled off her tongue like sweet honey. "Hi, I'm glad to meet you," I ventured. She held out a big farm girl's hand and I shook it. I thought about Grandmother and her theory that we never meet a stranger. I felt it applied here instantly. Char had beads braided into her hair, and a bell hung from a piece of leather around her neck.

Father arrived with the first bunch of my luggage. We introduced him and Mother gave him a list of stuff to get so that we could clean up the room. She added, "William, bring the girls some flowers too . . . something that smells good!" Father smiled and was off. Mother suggested that we take a little walk around the campus while we waited for the supplies. Char and I thought that a great idea so off we went. We visited the old clock tower. Mother told us that it had German clockworks inside; she said she read about it in a magazine. We found a little snack shop and bought a cold soda and chips. We ventured round like tourists, getting our bearings from the old tower, finally winding our way back around to the dorm where we found Father sitting on the steps.

We cleaned all afternoon. The room actually began to feel and smell a lot better. The dorm monitor came around to give us a list of house rules and told us that if we wanted, we could have dinner in the cafeteria with my folks. Mother and Father wanted to take Char and I out to dinner and we thought that would be more fun, so we set out to find a Chinese restaurant. We found a beautiful place called The Dynasty. We had dumplings, soup, and so much food that I thought we would burst. We laughed about the "dust bunnies" Mother pulled from under the dressers, and shared the fun of the cleanup with Father, who had gone to visit a professor friend while we got the room in order.

On the way back, Mother insisted that we stop at a mall. She said she just had to get some things for the room. She found a rug similar to mine for in front of Char's bed and when Char admired a comforter with bright, yellow flowers, she bought that too. Char was delighted and thanked her over and over.

Finally, we got back to the dorm. It was now a noisy place: parents leaving, radios blaring away. The dorm mom sat, looking exhausted, in an overstuffed chair in the commons room. My folks walked us up to our room and bid us goodnight. Mother hugged us both and whispered, "Be careful, dear. Don't get involved until you see what's what!" Father promised to come and get us on the second weekend. He and Mother wanted us to come to the house for a nice meal.

When at last they were gone, Char and I started to get the beds ready. She just couldn't get over the fact that Mother had bought her the rug and bed set. We finished making up our beds and suddenly the room took on a clean, new look!

"Your mother was right," Char said, standing back to look at our arrangement. "Putting the beds against the wall like that with the stand between them gives us a lot of room. They even look pretty now!" I had to agree; what a few hours before had looked like a tenement room now resembled a real bedroom, with room for growth!

Suddenly, there was a knock at our door. It startled us. We opened it to find the hall monitor and several other girls standing there. "Come down to room 210. We're going to have a first night party! We even got some beer." Char looked at me and I said simply, "We'll come down in a bit. We still have some things to unpack." This seemed to satisfy them and they made their rowdy way on down the hall to the next room.

"I don't really feel like a party, do you?" I ask Char. "Not me, not till I get to know people a bit," she stated flatly. I could tell that we were going to do okay. I had really wondered how it would feel to be put in a room with someone you didn't know. I was grateful that she was country folk. We finished putting all of our stuff away and took our suitcases out to the storage area in the hall. We were both full and tired; Char had come by plane from Mississippi that day, so we decided to call it a night. We found a nice station on the radio that played rock and roll, took our turns at the bathroom, then got into our beds. "Gosh, am I glad your mother bought me this pillow." Char said. "It's nice and soft." We talked quietly for a while about our families. I told Char I was born on a ship at the end of the Second World War. She didn't laugh. "My great-granny came here on a slave ship," she said.

We had just about drifted off to sleep when there was a loud noise out in the hall. Someone was banging on our door. "No sleeping! First night party! No one sleeps!!!" someone shouted at us. We decided that since the door was locked, we would just ignore them, but it was hard to get back to sleep. The last time I looked over at the clock, the hands read 11:00 P.M.

Morning came too soon. Both Char and I responded to the alarm with groans, but we both got right up and proceeded to get ready to go to orientation. We stopped at the cafeteria on the way, grabbed some juice and a muffin and then hurried on our way. The whole orientation process dragged on for hours. By the end of it, we were both starved. We had seen a hamburger spot just off the campus grounds and headed there to "fuel up," as Char put it. It was a Bob's, so of course we loaded ourselves with the Big Boy Burger, fries, and malts. We regained our energy and genuinely enjoyed ourselves. Again, our conversation turned to family and life at home. Char's mother was a cook at a restaurant and had saved enough money for Char to come here for two years. I applauded her stick—tuitiveness. Char was proud of her mom; she had been raised by her and her grandmother. As we began to share our stories, I could see that we were much alike in many ways. Char, too, was yet to have any serious affair with a young man and didn't seem in any hurry, so we made a pact: If either of us thought that some guy was trying to put the move on, we'd take the other out for dinner and a girl talk! I shared with her the difficulties that had come between my stepfather and me because of my activity back in Rapid.

"Ain't nothin', honey," Char said when I finished. "My granny, she refused to ride in the back of the bus, just like Mrs. Parks. And you know what? She changed a lot of things that way, not just for herself and mom and me, but for a lot of folks in the town where we live. I'm proud to be in the same room with you. There aren't many girls your age ever done anything yet and you been saving lives!" She reached over and gave me a tight hug. We were friends, and that was that!

Chapter XXI

Those first weeks at campus were tough. Char and I had different schedules and we were constantly on the move, so when Father arrived Friday noon to take us into San Francisco for the weekend, we were both more than ready. We took all our dirty clothes, our homework, of course and off we went.

Char had never been to San Francisco so Father took the slow route home through the city, down past Fisherman's Wharf, up through Chinatown. She oohed and aahed all the way. Mother was waiting for us at the house. Ann graciously relieved us of all responsibility for our dirty clothes and we went upstairs and got settled.

Mother decided that we needed a whole day off, so we planned to do the city on Saturday. But that evening, she and Father took us to the Russian Restaurant where Mother and I had gone. It was wonderful. We ate until we were satisfied, then sat and watched Mother and Father dance. "Your parents look so wonderful out there." Char commented. "I don't know if mom dances or not; she's always working." Father made the rounds with Char and I, even above her protests of not knowing how we were able to persuade her, and then we really had fun. There were several tables of young people and parents so soon we were getting asked to the dance floor by handsome young men who attempted to pretend they knew the old dances for the sake of the parents watching! We pretended pretty well, right around midnight. We had our last round of coffee and took our leave.

Father drove us home via the crookedest street in the world. Char and I got a fit of giggles and even Mother couldn't stop laughing. I couldn't remember ever having so much fun with my folks together! Saturday morning, we slept in then had a late breakfast and set out for Fisherman's Wharf. We did it all, every nook and cranny until around three, when Mother said we had to eat. We went to a posh place with tables that faced the water. I had crab cakes; Char ate a shrimp salad. She kept telling Mother and Father how grateful she was for this great treat, until Mother reached over and took her hand. "We have never had the opportunity to do this sort of thing together with Leah. It really is a pleasure for us and we thank you for coming!" Later, I told Char that I had never seen this side of my mother; that indeed, it was foreign to me and made me wonder why she hadn't liked me when I was little. "Maybe she did, but maybe she was too afraid that something would happen to take you away from her so she chose not to get attached." Char said, looking wise. "Truly, I've never thought about it that way," I answered. "I really just stopped expecting anything from her by the time I turned eight or so. I've really awful memories of the tenement building that we lived in when I was small. I can remember being cold, hungry and wet, with no one to take care of me. Now she seems so kind. I wish I knew everything that happened to her."

Char looked at me thoughtfully. "Have you ever asked? I mean, now that you are older, have you ever just asked?" "I have, but it has always turned out badly, and I don't want to lose what little closeness we have now," I answered. Char put her arm around my waist and we went on walking that way for a while until Father and Mother caught up to us. We went to tour the Gheradelli Chocolate Factory. When we got to the gift shop, Char saw a huge bar with nuts in it that was a "Post a Chocolate." She bought it and had the lady send it to her mom. I thought to myself, "All the places I've been without Mother and I never sent home anything." I felt sad inside. Looking at Char chatting with my mother over the items on display, I wished that I had.

We were tired, but Father had made reservations at a Chinese Restaurant, so off we went to dinner. The place was real China; plates of steaming dumplings disappeared right ahead of Mu Shu, followed by steaming, sizzling rice and great shrimp. Both Char and I ate like we were starving. Mother and Father giggled as they watched us consume plate after plate.

We ended the meal with a special dessert and headed for home. The drive was pleasant, the sun just beginning to set over the city streets. We passed a little flower shop just before the climb into the residential area where we lived and I noted the name, promising myself that I would send Mother a bouquet from there to thank her for the nice weekend.

We arrived at the house to find that Ann had set all our nice, clean clothes out on our beds, neatly folded and ready to pack. Problem was, we had brought them down in our pillow cases. I went to ask Mother if she could think of a way to get them back to the dorm in good fashion. "We'll get you both a laundry basket! That will do nicely!" she replied. Char and I had homework that needed attending, so we each went to our rooms and spent the hours of the long evening making sure that our grades would be pleasing. I didn't especially care for the job, but once I started I easily went on to finish. We met in the kitchen about 10:00 P.M., looking for a snack. Father heard us and came in from his study. "I know! Ice cream! Thirty-one-flavors!" he said, and off we went, Mother, Father, Char, and I to the nearest shop where we had double scoops all round: pralines and cream for me, double ripple chocolate for Mother, Rocky Road for Father and Strawberry Cheesecake for Char. What a strange sight we must have been to the counter boy, who had been about ready to close up. We were in a mix of clothes, which ranged from Father's fashionable smoking jacket and tweed trousers to my khaki jungle pants, as Mother called them.

It was a wonderful time. The air was crisp and fresh as we crawled back into the car. Suddenly, I remembered the times when Father would come to visit in the small, dingy apartment in New York, how we always did something together that was fun. But Mother didn't laugh or smile then as she did now. "Maybe," I thought to myself, "She needed time to heal the wounds of the past. Maybe that was why she was always crying. Maybe, now she is all right with it all." I knew that I still wouldn't open the subject, out of my own fear of losing the magic of the times we were sharing, out of my own need to have her approval.

The weekend went too fast. When Sunday afternoon approached, I was very sorry to have to go back. Char loved the house, the family, the fun we had. She thanked Mother and Father several times on the ride back to campus. Mother had gotten us each a nice wicker hamper for our clothes to go back in and so when we arrived at the dorm, Father helped us take them up. We bid him and Mother goodbye. They promised that this would be a once-a-month affair. We told them that we would mark our calendars and save up our appetites. We waved goodbye from the steps of the dorm until they were out of sight.

After we got our things put away and fresh linens on our beds, we decided to check out the kiosk in the quad to see if there was anything exciting going on. There were a lot of the usual things: concerts, club meetings, the stuff that fills the kiosks of college campuses of this country. But there was a notice: "SPECIAL EDITOR NEEDED, Please see Rex at Alpha Gamma Fraternity House. Must be open-minded, understand the crisis facing our nation and be actively against the situation in Vietnam." I tore off the telephone number and put it in my jeans pocket. "Remember, you're here to get educated!" Char cautioned. "Don't get involved!"

I didn't do anything right then, but when we got back to the dorm I put the number in my diary, in red ink. We got through the week quickly and had a long, three-day weekend ahead of us. We decided to see a movie on Friday with some of the other girls in our dorm. One of them was an open lesbian and the other an anti-war, anti-establishment protester who had already been warned by the campus powers-that-be.

Personally, I thought them both to be nice and actually welcomed the chance to be with someone who was aware of the things happening overseas. After the movie, we went for burgers at Bob's. The discussion quickly got around to Vietnam, and even when Char kicked me under the table, I got to find out where the next rally was going to be, and shared openly that I had helped some guys out by finding the "No Only Sons" clause. Anna, the anti-establishment girl, was from Milwaukee, Wisconsin. We hit it off right away and decided to go to the rally that Sunday together. Char gave me what for on the way back to the dorm, but finally said that secretly, she wanted to go too.

Sunday dawned bright and beautiful. The weather was crisp but the sky was clear. Char and I met Anna in the lobby of the dorm, signed out to "Go to the library," and headed across campus to the appointed rally site. There was a lot of hustle and bustle. We met friends of Anna's at the appointed place and got assigned to a small group who would pass petitions through the crowd, asking for signatures to send to Congress to protest our ever-increasing involvement in Vietnam. One of the guys in the group was introduced to us as "Rex." When we finally had our interactions down, he and I happened to head off in the same direction, so I took my chance. "Did you by any chance put a notice on the kiosk for an editor?" I asked quietly. "Yep!" he answered "You got any experience?" "I worked for our high school paper and our yearbook, but more importantly, I have experience with the Vietnam situation. I found a rule that keeps only sons from having to be drafted, and I helped my aunt and some other ladies get the word spread around back in Rapid, where I graduated high school." I said it all in one breath, hoping that he would take me seriously. It was a moment or two before I realized that he was standing there looking at me with his mouth hanging open. He finally recovered from my onslaught of information. "You are Elizabeth McRyan, aren't you?" he asked, as if stunned. I nodded, wondering how he knew my name. "I know about you.

They wrote about the women's group from South Dakota in the Congressional Register. They mentioned that a high school senior had found the rule and that now it was making a big stir in Washington." I blushed clear to my toes. I had no idea that what I'd done was news enough to reach here.

"Hey, Rob. Come over here. I want to introduce you to someone!" Rex shouted toward a tall, ruddy-faced young man in the midst of the crowd. He pushed his way toward us and Rex steered us off to an area by a large tree at the edge of the growing group. "This is the girl who found that "No First Sons" thing. Do you remember reading it?" "Remember! Hell, yes. I remember! I used it on my draft board this summer!" With that, he grabbed me and hugged me tight. "Hello, sweetheart!" he drawled. "My daddy hates you! You ruined a whole six-generation run of Army fools. I'll be the only Mobs never to serve his country!" He let go of me and took a long look. "And you're pretty as all dickens to boot!" he added. Rex told him that I was asking after the position on the paper. They decided that we'd meet after the rally and talk about it. My heart was drumming out a beat I didn't recognize, but I did love the way it felt, especially when I looked at Rob.

We spent the rest of that afternoon listening to music about no more wars, speakers who were grinding a big ax about the war, and gathering up as many signatures as we could on the petitions to Congress, demanding an explanation of our involvement and an immediate vote on the undeclared war that we were illicitly sending valuable young lives to. When it was over, we all met at the cafeteria, got a quick dinner and went out to the quad to discuss the paper. Char and Alexis headed back to the dorm while Anna, Rex, Rob, and I settled in for a serious chat.

The paper was an underground press, which was actually being published by the use of the Berkeley Stars' obsolete press. Rob had access because he worked part-time as a typesetter and the owner had agreed that as long as we did nothing illegal, we could use it. A family member of a famous publisher furnished all of our supplies, and our salaries were being paid for by a group of concerned citizens who thought that we had no business in the Vietnam thing. I decided that it was something that my father would be very angry over, but that I would take that risk because the truth needed to be told. The rest of the staff would have a meeting on Tuesday night down at the newspaper office and they would vote on whether to assign me as their editor.

When I got back to the dorm, Char looked like a thundercloud. She was sitting on her bed, cross-legged. "You aren't going to get involved, are you?" she asked. I explained to her that I was, and why. For a long while, she sat there staring. "I want to, too," she stammered suddenly. "But my mom would just never forgive me. My being here, this is her dream. She wants me to have the best education I can get. She and granny have struggled so hard to raise me. I can't let them down." She started to cry.

I went over and sat down next to her, handing her the box of Kleenex. "What if you just help me with the editing and we don't tell anyone, would that work?" I asked. She shook her head sadly. "You know my granny, she done a lot of stuff when all the segregation things were going on. I want to *do* something that makes a *difference*. I want to be a *part* of it!" "We'll figure out a way," I promised, not knowing how. "We'll work on it. There's got to be some way for you to do what you want and not get into any kind of trouble." "What about you? You know your stepfather is gon' disown you if you do one thing more! You'll be sorry, Elizabeth. I don't want you to have a problem with your father. I don't want to cause my mom or my granny no grief either! What can we do?" I admitted that I didn't know, but that I couldn't sit here and do nothing. It just wasn't my nature to let things go. "We'll wait and see what the group does when they meet. Maybe someone won't want me or there will be someone better who'll come along before Tuesday. Let's not think about it until then." Char agreed and we put the issue away for a while. I could tell that she was a real good daughter. I don't think I gave that a second thought when I got involved back in Rapid. In fact, I know that I didn't think of Father's feelings or his reaction at all; I just plowed my way through like a bull in a china closet!

❧ Chapter XXII

Life on campus moved swiftly. It was Tuesday afternoon before I could think. Rob found me just outside the Music Building to tell me that the group had voted me in as the new editor of their underground press. I didn't know whether I should be happy or go back to my dorm and start packing. "What are the chances that my folks could find out about my involvement?" I asked pensively. "One in a million years!" Rob answered confidently. "We don't exactly have a circulation in the city. We only send out copies to guys who are looking for ways to be saved from the draft. You haven't got a brother in that category so I wouldn't worry." It made me feel easier about the whole thing, but inside I had the hunch that Father had other ways of keeping tabs on me. I certainly hoped that I was wrong. I accepted the offer and was put right to work that evening, when Rex dropped off the plot of the front page for this week's edition. I pored over it, looking for errors in grammar and spelling but mostly looking for anything that I thought could hurt us. Char was quiet and I could tell that she was worried. "It's okay," I assured her. "Our circulation is very tight; we only send it to people that subscribe or ask for a copy." She didn't look as if she believed me but nodded affirmatively in my defense.

We went on with our normal routine of classes. I attended to my job at the press with pride and confidence, and I liked the group. Everyone was super-intelligent and no one found fault with each other. It was pleasant and I felt fortunate to be involved. The third Friday of the month was coming up and Father was to come up for us so we could spend a weekend at home. I had a conflict. There was going to be a rally late in the afternoon that day and I desperately wanted to go. One of the speakers was very important to our movement and it would look odd if I didn't show up. I made a decision to ask Father to come on about five, but as I dialed the number, I got cold feet. He would ask for an explanation because he knew my schedule, and what would I say? I certainly couldn't tell him that I was going to a rally without telling him what it was about. I put down the phone and sat staring into space, trying to gather the courage to be honest without giving myself away.

Char came in while I was still sitting there. She could tell by the look on my face that I was dealing with the situation, but not doing well. "Listen to yourself; pay attention to how you feel inside," she cautioned me. "Remember, if you lie, you have to live with it." I tried to think about what my grandmother would do. I thought that if I tried hard enough, I could make this a lie of conscience, but the more I thought about it, the more I knew it wouldn't work! My father would figure it out and I'd be in deep water. In the end, I decided that I would just have to miss the rally and someone else would have to take my place. I went out and found Rex to ask him if he thought he could cover for me. He was studying in the library when I finally located him. "Why can't you be there?" he asked quietly. When I had told him the problem, to my surprise, he thought that it was wise for me to go on with my plans with my folks. The whole thing took me by surprise, but he explained that the group always covered for each other and it was no big thing! I rushed back to the dorm to let Char know that for this time, it was settled and I wouldn't have to figure out a way to deal with Father. "Next time it might not be that easy," was all she said. I could tell that it bothered her to think that I had contemplated lying to my father.

The weekend came and we went into the city and had a great time. My mother took us both shopping for spring clothes and was gracious and generous with Char. It never ceased to amaze me how much different she was now that I was nearly grown. I still held my questions in, though, because it never seemed like quite the time to ask. Father was not his usual self and right before we were to leave to go back up to campus, he called me to his study to ask me about what I was doing with my spare time. I never mentioned the paper and he never asked, but I had the feeling that he was watching me somehow, and waiting to see if I got my head together and quit. He waltzed all around the main issue, and at the end of our conversation, he showed me an article in the news that said how things were "heating up" on the campus at Berkley, and other places too. He looked at me sternly and leaning forward, said, "Do you recall what I told you last fall when the semester started?" I nodded. He looked at me for a moment and proceeded, "Leah, I won't tolerate you having any involvement with the anti-war movement. The first time that I think you have, I'll take steps to see to that you can't embarrass me or your mother. Do we have that clear?" I wanted to ask him what it was he would do, but I stopped myself. I really didn't want to know. I felt threatened, I felt sad, I felt frightened. All the way back to campus, I kept hearing him say, "I'll take steps." That night, I wrote to my Tante Rivka a long, sad letter, telling her what I was doing and why I thought that it was right. I wrote to Grandmother, too. I remember that she always told me that one must stand up for what they believe. Desperately, I needed her support against Father, and I wanted to know if he had told her his plan for me if I embarrassed him.

I couldn't sleep well; I lay awake for hours staring up at the ceiling, trying to still myself, trying to quiet the cacophony of fear that was playing itself out in my head. I was still awake when the first light of morning graced our windows. Char was up already so I climbed out of bed, made myself a cup of strong instant coffee and was sitting there sipping it when she came back from her shower. "You didn't sleep," she stated. "You shouldn't worry so much. Remember, your father isn't G-d. It's not like he can spy on you. If you can't stand it, maybe you should quit the paper." Dear Char, she was simple! Everything to her had a simple answer. I expect that was how her mother ran her life, too, very simple and uncomplicated. Normal, I thought to myself.

Good, normal, Christian folk who never got involved if it meant having conflicts. "I can't simply quit, it goes against my very being," I told her, picking up my towel and heading for the shower. "Besides that, I don't want to. If Father is going to do something outrageous, then I may as well make my involvement worthwhile."

Standing in the hot shower, letting the water beat on my body, I decided that no matter what, I was going to make a difference, and if my stepfather wanted to punish me for being myself, then maybe I really never knew him at all. Maybe he was two-faced, treating me one way while treating outsiders another. That day was a turning point in my growing up. I knew that I would act my conscience, no matter what the consequences were. I knew that I would defend my right and the right of others to speak their mind in private and in public. I realized that there were serious political, social, and economic issues at stake in the war in Vietnam. I also knew that already, too many young men had been ripped out of the prime of their lives and sent off to die for a cause that none of us could understand. As I toweled myself dry that day, I knew Father would make good on his threat but until that last moment, I would voice my opinions and work for the cause. When I arrived at the paper's office that afternoon, the headers on the front page looked like any other paper in America. I reworded it until there was little doubt it was a statement of truth. When the paper went to the press, it read, "No More Only Sons! No Sons at All!" And the editorial article that followed listed all the reasons why I and hundreds of other college-age students were marching in the streets against the war which had never officially been declared. Everyone loved my article; the stacks of papers disappeared in record time and we were forced to run a second printing the next day. Now I was really involved. I no longer just edited others' words and thoughts; I was putting my own in print. It felt great!

A letter arrived from Grandmother. "You must serve your conscience," she told me. "Mason Lake has already lost one-half of its young men," she wrote, and included a clipping from the *Daily* which stated that "This war in Vietnam has already taken away more youth from our small town than both world wars combined!" I quoted that article in our next edition, and I quoted my grandmother's words to me. In a few days, the largest rally against the war so far was scheduled in the city. I was going. In fact, our whole staff intended to drive up on Saturday morning. We were marching on the second largest draft center in the United States.

My afternoons were filled with helping to structure signs and banners against the war. I wasn't involved in the radical, destructive side of things, but in the more peaceful and vocal end of the protests. Char and I hadn't been spending much time with each other so I was shocked to find her at the meeting place for the vans on Saturday. I was even more shocked to see that the girls she was with were the ones whom the rest of us worried about, the more radical element of protests who had done things in the past, like chain themselves to the post in front of the draft center to prevent the people who ran the place from coming to work! She had on a pair of khaki trousers and a heavy belt. She wore a camouflage shirt and her hair was tied back under a red bandanna. I went over to her, "What are you doing here?" I asked quietly. "I'm going to make a difference too!" she replied, looking straight into my eyes. "I'm tired of sitting still while the whole world moves on!" I wanted to drag her away from the group she was with. I tried to persuade her to come with us on the bus that the rest of the staff were on. She refused. "I found my own niche. I like the ideas of this whole group," she replied, letting my caution fall on deaf ears.

All the way into the city I thought about Char. She was so

simple that I just couldn't believe the group she was with. Maybe she chose them because she didn't realize how radical they were, I told myself. Maybe I can catch up with her again when we arrive and persuade her to come with us. Maybe I can remind her of her mom . . . maybe?

There were already hundreds of youth in the streets and nearby parks when our vans arrived. We joined the group that was getting ready to march the twin six blocks to the Draft Center. I never had a chance to try to find Char. When next I saw her, she was chained together with three other girls, blocking the driveway to the parking lot of the Center.

We chanted as we walked. Older people yelled at us and all along the way, there were police and what appeared to be National Guardsmen. There were news cameras and flash cameras taking shots of everything. When we reached the Draft Center, somewhere in the crowd, a loud explosion sounded. The police began to push us back toward the direction we had come from. It wasn't until several hours later that we learned that someone from the PLO had set off a bomb in the rear of the building. Luckily, no one was seriously injured, but a lot of young men and women went to jail that day. Char was among them. I had to borrow a car and take money from my school account to go and bail her out. She was like a madwoman. As we drove off from the police station, she shouted out the window, "No more! We won't take it anymore!"

That night, I watched as the news media had their field day with the events that had taken place. More than once I saw myself in the pictures. I knew that by morning, Father would have too. Now all I could do was wait.

Char's mother called about 11:00 P.M. She had come in from work to see her daughter's face on TV. "What were you thinking?" I could hear her shouting at Char, whose face was white as if she were a ghost. "Mama, I had to do something. I had to make a difference! Why can't you understand?" Finally, Char was quiet and I could no longer hear her mother shouting. "Yes, Mama," Char said over and over. "I'm sorry, Mama," she said at last, hanging up the phone. I didn't know what I would say when my turn came. I didn't know if I would be able to say I was sorry.

Char and I sat up far into the night, talking about the events of the past months. She shared with me what it was that made her so angry that she joined the radical group. She showed me clippings from the papers in the South where they claimed more young men were being drafted than in other places. I talked to her about there being less radical ways, about Gandhi, about Martin Luther King, until finally she began to cry. "I just wanted so much to do something!" she said, tears streaming. "I wanted to be brave like you!" I felt responsible; I felt afraid for my friend. "What did you promise your mother?" I asked after a while. "I told her that I wouldn't do anything more if she will just forgive me and let me stay here," Char told me, looking more pitiful than before. "Trouble is, I don't know if I can just quit." "You can join our group. You can write for the press or be a reporter," I suggested. We sat through the night, waiting for the inevitable phone call from my father, but it didn't come. Perhaps he hadn't seen the news, I thought hopefully.

Morning came. Our dorm mother called all of us who had gone to the rally to a meeting in her office. We were put on official notice that if any of us violated the rules of conduct in the dorm or made a public nuisance of ourselves again, we would be expelled from the dorm and just possibly, from the campus. We were subdued; all of us wanted to go out and find out how the others who had gone were faring in their dorms, but we were confined to our dorm until further notice. In other words, until the dean came in on Monday and decided what should be done.

Char, I, and several others of the girls who had gone were sitting in the commons room when the door opened. There stood my father. His face was a veritable storm cloud. Walking over to me, he said simply, "Go pack your things." I started to protest but thought that it would do more harm than good. "Where am I going?" I asked plaintively. "You have an hour. Go pack," was his only reply. Char and several of the other girls helped me. I decided only to take my personal things and my clothing. Little did I know how much I would need some of the things I left behind. My mind was whirling; I couldn't imagine what he had in mind. The hour sped by. I don't know where my father spent it but he reappeared at the door to our room exactly as the hands moved into the tenth hour. Without speaking, he began to carry out my things. He never even looked at me; he just picked up the luggage and headed down the hall.

Char and I clung to each other. "You'll be back," she whispered. I wasn't sure about that. My stepfather had never acted this way toward me, so uncaring and determined. Once in the car, I tried to talk to him. I begged him to tell me what he was doing, where I was going. He drove in silence. After we left the usual route toward home, I became terribly frightened. When we turned off the freeway toward the airport, I was terrified! "What did I do that was so awful?" I asked again and again, finally breaking down in tears from the stress of the whole affair. "Where are you taking me?" I begged. As we arrived in the parking area for the international flights, he reached into the pocket of his coat. Silently, he handed me my passport and an airline ticket. "San Francisco to Tel Aviv," I read. "Am I going to Tante Rivka?" I asked. He only stared at me in silence. We took my bags and gave them to a skycap. My stepfather took me by the elbow and steered me toward the gate number on my ticket. His grip was hard and felt unkind. "I warned you," he said simply. The overhead announcement for first boarding came over the speakers. He literally pushed me forward toward the gate. "Does Mother know you are doing this?" I pleaded. No answer, just his steely gaze, the same one that he had given to the customs agent the day we had the problem. When we finally reached the gate, Father handed me over like a five-year-old to a stewardess. "Don't let her get off the plane," he said simply, handing the ticket to her. "A Rabbi by the name of Haim Lakov will meet her at the gate in Tel Aviv." He added and before I could ask another question, he had turned away and was walking back toward the exit. "Father!" I called after him "Father! Please!" But it was no use; the stewardess now had a grip on my arm and we were moving down the loading ramp toward the plane's door. Once inside, she didn't leave me but sat in the seat next to mine. It didn't take long for me to realize that she had been hired to stay with me the whole trip.

I felt totally bereft. How could this person who had always been so kind and caring toward me suddenly turn so harsh and uncaring? Did Mother know where I was headed? Did she approve? Did Tante Rivka know? Would I see her? My head ached, my heart pounded in my ears and I felt sick. I had always been a good traveler but now I was ill. I threw up until I couldn't throw up anymore. Finally exhausted, I fell asleep.

When I awoke, at first I thought that I had had a nightmare, but it wasn't so. I was still seated next to the stewardess and we were fast approaching the runway in Tel Aviv.

The stewardess let me go to the washroom to freshen up. When I came back, she handed me a heavy envelope. Inside was a note from my mother explaining that I was being sent to Kibbutz Yad Mordechai at her request; that I shouldn't be upset with Father, he was only protecting me and our family. Mother wrote that I would receive a stipend each month for my own personal use — $800.00 — and that the necessary money for my upkeep would be paid directly to the kibbutz. My first month's check was enclosed along with a medical aid card issued through the U.S. Embassy so that if I had anything come up physically, it would be taken care of at the local U.S. medical building. There was another small envelope attached which said on the outside, "Wait to open this." I put everything back in the envelope and shoved it into my purse.

My fright was giving way to anger, tremendous grief mingled with it, as if I had lost my Father forever. I felt totally betrayed! I made up my mind that he would never influence my life again. I didn't know how I would do it but I promised myself that I would find a way back to the U.S., and that I would go to school on my own. I also decided that I wouldn't write or call no matter how hard things got! The plane landed late and the Rabbi was waiting. He seemed a nice fellow who spoke moderately decent English. After getting my bags, we found our way out of the building onto a bus that was waiting. It appeared just for us. I was silent, sadly wrapped up in my own feelings at first. Slowly, I tried to quiet my thoughts until I finally was able to look out the window and feel the impact of what had taken place.

The Rabbi was seated across from the driver and they were conversing quietly in Hebrew. I leaned forward and asked, "Please, could you tell me where it is that we are going?" The Rabbi answered politely that I was on my way to Yad Mordechai, a kibbutz on the southern edge of Israel. He didn't volunteer anything else, so I returned to my gazing out the window, trying to meditate away the pain that engulfed me.

Finally, we arrived and I was ushered into a large room with several desks where a nurse gave me a once-over, while a beautiful young lady several years my senior began the task of instructing me in the life of the Kibbutz. After what seemed an endless lecture, I was asked if I had any questions. "Just one," I replied, trying to remember my grandmother's rule about mutual respect. "Do you often take in young Americans under these circumstances?" "Which circumstances are you referring to?" she asked politely. "I was sent here by my stepfather; it was against my wishes," I answered. "Does that happen often?" "No, not often, but only when one needs to learn that there are boundaries in life."

"Ah, is that it?" I mused half aloud, half to myself. My stepfather thinks that I will learn to be a good little sheep if I am forced to live the life here for a while. That here, I will learn to follow the leaders without question, to not make ripples in the pool of life, I thought rather than spoke.

"I expect you are hungry. Your companion told us you were ill on the flight, so if you will come with me to the kitchen we will find something for you to eat," the young lady said, rising and heading toward the door.

I followed her, thinking to myself that this was another life, a world away from everything I had ever known and that it would test my own endurance to the point of near-breaking, but that I would never give up, nor give in. The ordeal was to be survived! Just as I had all my life until now. Just as my mother and my aunt had managed to survive, so would I.

I Am My Mother's Memory 199

Chapter XXIII

In the beginning, life on the Kibbutz seemed foreign. I felt a terrible homesickness and was often ill. The people were kind and caring. All the Sabras were truly beautiful; they had everything that any girl could wish for in looks, body shape, and hair. But more than that, they all seemed to be genuine, real, none of the superficial stuff that we in America practiced so commonly. When they cared, it was a deep and discerning interest. I soon began to feel closer to many of them than I had to anyone in my life except Tante Rivka.

We all worked hard. Up at first light, there was much to do: animals that needed tending to, crops that needed weeding or picking or thinning, and always the one hundred and one other jobs that are necessary to sustain life without the assistance of modern technology or supermarkets. The Rabbitzin an was a lovely woman who mothered all of us. She was amazed when I took over the job of squeezing the milk from the bags of cheese that were forming in the great dairy room. She asked how I had learned to do it, and when I shared my stories of the lake and Grandmother, she looked at me and said, "Are you sure she isn't one of us?"

I got used to being there, but not to being without family. Eventually, I broke my own rule about contact and called my Tante Rivka. The connection was poor but her voice brought tears to my eyes that spilled over to my face. I leaned against the hard wood of the booth and sobbed, unable to talk. She said simply, "I'll come to see you." Several days passed and there she was, descending from the steps of the bus like an angel! I ran to her arms and she held me fast for a long while. When at last I regained my composure, I began to introduce her to all of my Kibbutz Family. To my surprise, she knew the Rabbi and his wife! She said, "I forced your stepfather to tell me where you were. He made me promise that I wouldn't rescue you in return for the information. I had a very hard time not allowing myself to come straight out here and take you home with me," she smiled, but tears brimmed in her eyes. "I told him that if he was so ashamed of you being a mench, he should have let me take you!"

After her first visit, she came whenever she could to check up on me. I adjusted to the visits and told myself that this, too, would pass. Grandmother wrote nearly every week; that helped too. She was so angry with my father that she was no longer communicating with him. In her strong, plain pen, she wrote, "This country was founded on the belief that all of humanity had a right to speak up; to be whoever they wanted; to fight for what they believed in. Your grandfather would hate what William has done. He would have disowned him for being so harsh with you!" After a while, she stopped even mentioning Father. Our letters were full of what she was doing, how the sleepy little town was or with questions about how I was faring.

One morning, we were awakened before dawn to the sound of explosions off in the distance, loud noises resounding off the wall of the Wadi. Israel was at War! Before the sun had risen, soldiers appeared in the barracks, asking if any of us knew how to shoot a rifle. My grandmother and my uncles had taught me and so I raised my hand. One of the soldiers took me outside, handed me a large American Army rifle and told me to shoot at some tins sitting on the wall. I took aim and fired, knocking them off one at a time.

"Very good," he said, smiling. "You are now conscripted to the Israeli Army." That was that! Here I was at the edge of the desert, at war. The girl who had been an anti-war activist now became a soldier. No training, just given the gun and told that I would defend to the death the people of Israel, our homeland itself, and the beliefs of our people. It wasn't hard to accept the challenge put to me by a handsome young lieutenant with thick, dark curls and deep, hazel-colored eyes. He looked at me sternly as he asked if I accepted my duties. I looked him straight in the eye and answered, "Yes, sir. With pride, sir." There were seventeen of us. We were all teens, and about half of us were girls.

There were no formal instructions, no uniforms and no pomp or circumstance, just the simple question of acceptance of duty and our replies. For the first time in my life, I felt both an awesome pride at being fit to do such a task, and the deep humbling that comes with the knowledge that you must defend what you believe.

There were half a dozen or so regular soldiers who stayed with us for the duration of the short but bloody war. The young lieutenant who swore me in was in charge. On the second day, when the sounds of the tanks and guns had become a constant din in the near distance, we heard that there were troops who were advancing toward us and that we would probably need to evacuate the kibbutz. Lt. Avrim had gone up a sandy hill with his binoculars to see if the enemy was within sight. Suddenly, above the din, a single loud shot rang out. The lieutenant fell backwards. From my vantage point, it seemed to be in slow motion. Then without a thought, I lay down my weapon and sprinted for the hill! I could see his eyes in front of me as they had been when he swore me in: proud, strong, and demanding. When I reached him, I could see that his leg was bleeding badly. I grabbed him by his boots and somehow managed to pull him from the top of the hill down to a position where others could come to our assistance. To this day, I don't know how I did it, or what the force was within me that made me act in such a fast, unthinking fashion. He lived, and I was given a Medal of Heroism by the government of Israel. I didn't feel as if I had done anything that anyone else wouldn't have, but according to my kibbutz family, I had!

Wars of any type are hard, but war in the desert of Israel is fast and furious. Almost before we could adjust our thinking to accommodate it, it ended. Personally, I learned more about myself in that short week than I had ever known before. I came to understand that not all war is avoidable, that serving one's conscience can be done as easily in the grip of a terrifying moment as when you have time to think over what you want to do. The most important lesson that I learned from those days was that strength rises up in you like a river flood just when you need it, when you least expect it. And that no matter where you may find yourself in life, the basic person that you are will show itself. I learned that life prepares us for whatever we might face, and that nothing you learn along the way is purposeless; everything fits into the puzzle right where it belongs, either making you a hero or a coward, strong or weak, sure-footed or lame. The whole thing is dependent on how you deal with the moment when it comes.

My Tante Rivka came out as soon as it was safe to travel. She was astonished when the Rabbi told her what I had done. I'll never forget the look on her face: pride, mingled with love that made her eyes water and her chin lift upward. She looked at me in silence for a long while. "A hero," she said. "My child . . . a hero." Everyone in the family looked up to me. The littlest of the children all wanted to be in my barracks. Suddenly, my position of being a foreigner and being sad changed. It felt good! No, it was wonderful! I really knew myself. I was no longer the injured child of my past; I was a person who was capable of life-and-death decisions, capable of being who I was intended to be, and I was proud that I was in the kibbutz. Proud to have served the country. Proud that I had volunteered.

I don't know if my stepfather inquired after me when the war broke out. I don't even know if he inquired afterward. Tante Rivka said that she cabled Mother so that she would not worry, but we didn't discuss Father.

I would spend another six months there, but now I formed a plan. I had not used any of the money that came each month and as a result, I had been able to save about 8,000 U.S. dollars. I began to plan a return to the United States without my stepfather's knowing! I sent off for information about Juilliard, the music school that I had so much wanted to attend in New York. I began to use my spare time in the evening to work on a plan on how to get a plane ticket and, once back in the States, how to survive. I ordered a once-a-week subscription to the *New York Times*.

Even though the paper arrived a week after the fact, I was able to get a fair idea of how much it would cost to live in the city, and even was able to formulate a vague idea of where I might find a small, inexpensive, and furnished apartment.

I was careful not to let anyone know what I was planning and didn't even mention it to my grandmother when I wrote because I didn't want her to have to lie to Father. The idea of being home in the States made me feel in control. I really felt that I could manage now by myself, without my stepfather or his interference.

When my plan finally had time to jell, I asked to be allowed to go to Jerusalem for High Holidays to spend it with my Tante Rivka. The Rabbi and his wife treated me with the respect that comes with age. They thought that the request was valid and had no problem arranging for me to catch the bus. So on a gorgeous bright morning in the early light, I boarded a bus bound for Tel Aviv, where I could transfer to another and eventually wind my way to Jerusalem. I took most of my clothes, some pictures, and other mementos, but nothing that might make anyone suspicious about whether I intended to return. I said good-bye to the family I had grown to love, and took flight.

I spent about ten days with Tante Rivka, sometimes wandering into the city on my own. I was able to find a travel agent who secured a ticket to New York for me, and so on the last Wednesday of September, I boarded the bus, headed back to Tel Aviv and got off the first time it stopped. I made my way back to the international airport, passed through the customs gate without any problems, and boarded a plane bound for New York. I was free!

Chapter XXIV

When my feet touched ground in New York, I felt at once lonely and elated. My plan had gone smoothly and I had not told a living soul so that now it seemed I was free. Free from the restraints of my stepfather, free from the mother who didn't love me. But suddenly, in the middle of the airport, I was stopped cold in my thinking. What of those who did love me? My dear Tante Rivka – my mother? My grandmother? All of those who had aided me in the process of growing up? I sat down on a nearby planter and began to weep. What had I done? They would all start looking for me by sunrise tomorrow, when I wouldn't appear at the bus stop near my kibbutz. I hadn't thought all of that through; I had acted as if it didn't matter and in my haste, I had erred in my reasoning. What to do? I sat there for a while, thinking that maybe I should call my grandmother or Tante Rivka, just so they would know that nothing awful had happened. If I did call, my mind reasoned, then either I would have to ask them to lie for me or . . . I couldn't! What was done was done! Here I was with a plan, with money, and right at this moment, what I needed to do was get out of this very public place and try to register at a hotel somewhere for the night. I needed privacy to think about my next action.

I hailed a cab and had them take me to the Village. I had decided from the papers that I'd read that it was an easy place to find a small apartment. I also knew that the small, old Essex Hotel was clean and traveler friendly to young people.

The taxi sped across town and I remembered why I didn't like big cities: the noise, the rushing about, the crush of people and automobiles, descended in lightning speed into my otherwise disturbed brain and for a minute or two, I felt the worst panic I had ever known. Why didn't I go to Kirabashi? I asked myself.

We arrived and gratefully, the little sign in the window read "Vacancy–Single Only." I paid my cab driver and ran up the steps into the lobby. An old, white-haired lady was dusting a table near the registration desk. I startled her with my entrance. "Yes?" she said, moving slowly back behind the old, mahogany counter. "What might I do for you?" I could smell the faint odor of lilacs and tried to smile at her before I answered. She took out a pen, lay it on a slip of paper that read Registration Card, and pushed the two toward me. "Are you here to see America?" she asked, taking off her tiny spectacles to reveal a deep-set pair of blue-green eyes which may have looked better on a cat. "Do you speak English?" She asked when I didn't answer. "Yes, oh yes," I stammered. "It's $7.50 a night. You pay as you go or by the week, it's only $50.00. There's no men allowed, no smoking in the rooms, no hot plates, and no radios."

I thought for a moment and took out a $100 bill. She looked at it real close and then at me "One week or two?" she queried. "Two," I managed. "You don't talk much, do you?" she commented as she wrote out a receipt. "I am just very tired. I just got off a plane." I tried to be polite. "Where did you come from?" she asked, her backed turned to me as she took a key from the board. I chose not to answer and she didn't pursue it. "Here, this is the only key so if you lose it, you pay $8 bucks and I'll get you another. You never take it out of the building with you. You turn it in so the maid can do up your room. You get fresh sheets every other day and towels every day. There's a fresh bar of soap in the room on the sink. You get one a month," she handed me the key. "Room seventeen, second floor. Upstairs, on the front," she motioned toward the stairs. "The elevator don't work." I headed in the direction she'd motioned. "If you want to come back down after you're settled, I've got fresh coffee and some cinnamon buns." "Thanks," I hollered back. The room was clean. The window opened into the fire escape and a little breeze came through. There was a bed, two overstuffed chairs with a little table between and a lamp next to a small desk. I noted that this was the first time I had ever been alone anywhere, ever registered at a hotel. This was actually the first place I had ever been where there wasn't a familiar adult next door or just down the hall. It felt strange and suddenly, I realized that I had acted like an adult, but with none of the necessary experience to help me get on. I promised myself that I would make it.

I unpacked my bags, washed my face, and combed my hair. I still needed to decide what to do about telling someone I was all right, but that could wait. There was an interesting old lady downstairs with coffee and cinnamon buns, and that seemed like a good idea. As she set out steaming cups of fresh-smelling coffee and a plate full of yummy-looking cinnamon buns, she twittered on about the city, about what a great, big melting pot it was and how she had come here from Iowa at sixteen and been here ever since. She seemed content to just talk about herself and since she didn't ask any questions, I didn't have to wonder what to say. The buns were wonderful, the coffee great, and when at last she paused in her story, I asked, "Do you know where Juilliard is from here?" "Juilliard," she smiled. "Of course, I know. Finish your coffee and I'll take you there. I have to go get some things at the store anyhow." I objected, but when she was insistent, I gave in.

She drove right to it. I was amazed. "You really know your way around," I ventured. "Sure, honey," she replied. "My husband taught here for thirty years. Most of the girls in the house either go here or wish they did. You are going to go to school here?" "I hope to," I told her. "I play the piano and I would like to be a concert pianist, even though my stepfather says that no one makes a living from music." "Ah, that's how it is then," she looked at me solemnly. "You ran away, did you?" I didn't answer and she didn't repeat the question.

We drove clear around the building twice while she told me who to see and which door to use. We went to a small market in the village then and I helped her with the bags of groceries. "Seems like a lot of food," I said. "Do you only shop once a week?" "Heavens, no!" she chuckled. "All of the girls near starve even if they have work, so I fix dinner every night and whoever shows up in the dining room can eat. All I ask is that you drop a little something in the charity box on the serving table whatever you can spare, even if it's only a dime."

We drove back to the hotel in silence. She hummed to herself while I enjoyed the sights. I helped her in with her things and went up to my room. I lay across the bed and stared up at the ancient ceiling, wondering what to do. I reasoned that one phone call should put everything at rest, and after thinking about what to say and who to call, went down to the lobby phone booth and dialed my grandmother. She listened as always, "I am not surprised," she said. She told me to leave it to her. She didn't ask where I was, only if I was safe and made me promise to call once a week so she could know I was okay. I agreed. When I came out of the phone booth, I felt like a great weight had been lifted off my shoulders. I could smell something cooking that rang a note of familiarity in my soul. I rang the ancient call bell on the desk and the little lady appeared. "I don't know your name," I stammered. "Alma," she replied and added, "Last names don't matter unless they're in lights on Broadway." I thanked her for the kindness of the morning, and her eyes softened. "You'll be all right, kid. You'll see. It's only hard for a while, then you get used to it. And here you are going to school and working and doing the things those girls your age do. It will all work out, whatever the trouble is." She reached over the counter to pat my hand.

I believed she was right, it would all work out. The panic of the morning was gone completely and now I was tired. I went up and lay down for the first time on a bed of my own choosing. I had achieved my goal, and I was satisfied that everything would work out just as I had planned.

I Am My Mother's Memory 211

GBP